"Wendy Weiss honed her skills in New York City—If you can cold call there, you can cold call anywhere. New York City is the toughest market in the world. Her techniques are simple, easy to follow, and (here's the best part)—they work!"

> Jeffrey Gitomer
> Author of *The Sales Bible* and coauthor of
> *Knock Your Socks Off Selling*

"If you shudder at the thought of making cold calls, the ideas and inspiration in this book will transform your fear into enthusiasm, your reluctance into results."

> Robert Bly
> Author of *Secrets of Successful Telephone Selling*

"This book is overflowing with insights and practical ideas. Whether you are a beginner or a seasoned professional, *Cold Calling for Women* will at a minimum double your cold-calling success rate."

> Fred Gleeck
> Marketing Consultant, Author of the
> soon-to-be-released *The Home-Based Business
> Marketing Manual*

"We thoroughly enjoyed your approach to cold calling—viewing phone work as a performance that needs constant practice and rehearsal. Prior to this, many of us viewed cold calling simply as a chore! Thank you."

> Kathleen Healy Englehart
> Director/President
> Long Island Women's Network

"Sometimes getting in to see a prospect is like getting in to see Oz. Wendy's techniques have opened doors that were previously closed and inaccessible."

> James Benard
> President, Match

"Your techniques have given me the confidence I need to approach potential clients via the telephone and I have overcome my fear of making cold calls! I am gaining new clients every week thanks to your techniques."

> Cathy Schwartz
> Vice President
> PHunPHit Custom Apparel & Promotions

"I know that the success of our company is tied directly to the success of our sales force. In today's competitive market-place you have to make sure your sales force has all the skills necessary to compete. Wendy Weiss's training program gave our sales team the skills and confidence they needed to succeed. Our company's sales are now far exceeding my expectations. Thanks, Wendy!!"

> Bridget Pucheu
> Vice President
> Messages Plus Corporation

"I have totally overcome my fear of cold calling. I now have a 100 percent success rate on a cold call! If prospecting is a part of your job, drop everything now and read this book! Then follow the steps. They work."

> Lynda Decker
> Decker Design, Inc.

"I have had tremendous success utilizing Wendy's techniques for ferreting out and getting through to proper contact people as well as performing in a persuasive and effective manner once I get there. I would recommend her clear and forceful program to anyone who needs to learn how to get proven sales results."

> Dean Villella
> Director of Institutional Operations
> Messages Plus Corporation

"Your cold calling program was inspirational.... You provided me with the motivation to make those calls...."

> John Barry
> Vice President
> Oliver Staffing, Inc.

"Wendy increased our sales by training my staff with a realistic and practical approach to cold calling and telephone sales."

> Lawrence Peters
> Managing Director of Special Marketing
> Hachette Filipacchi Magazines

"Wendy is terrific. She has really helped our business grow!"

> John Kneapler
> President
> John Kneapler Design

Cold Calling for Women

for Women

OPENING DOORS & CLOSING SALES

Wendy Weiss

Foreword by
Dottie Walters sales expert, author of *Never Underestimate the Selling Power of a Woman* and coauthor of *Selling Women*

D.F.D.
publications
new york

Published by:
D.F.D. Publications, Inc.
P.O. Box 20664
London Terrace Station
New York, New York 10011

Cover design: Foster & Foster, Inc.
Author photo: Mike Tauber

Publisher's Cataloging-in-Publication Data
(Provided by Quality Books, Inc.)

Weiss, Wendy.
    Cold calling for women . opening doors &
closing sales / Wendy Weiss -- 1st ed.
    p. cm.
    LCCN: 99-95694
    ISBN: 0-9671268-0-0

    1. Telephone selling. 2. Telemarketing.
3. Women sales personnel.   I. Title.

HF5438.3.W45 2000   658.85
                    QBI99-1482

Printed in the United States of America

10 9 8 7 6 5

*There is a vitality, a life force, an energy, a
quickening, that is translated through you
into action, and because there is only one of
you in all time, this expression is unique.
And if you avoid it, it will be lost.*

Martha Graham

Contents

Acknowledgments

I am very grateful to the many people who encouraged and assisted me with this project. I would never have written *Cold Calling for Women* without their help.

I owe a special thank you to Fred Gleeck, who told me to write this book. I then went home and wrote it! His inspiration was the beginning of this entire project.

I want to thank Cynthia Nadelman for patiently and precisely copy editing this book. I must also thank Michael Collins, James Edwin Parker, Mark Puttre, Cathy Schwartz and Leslee Weiss for reading, brainstorming and making much-needed comments, suggestions and improvements on the manuscript.

I am grateful to Sharon Good for her advice on publishing and for helping me to stay calm when the detail work became too much. Many thanks to Dan Poynter for his advice on publishing and marketing—along with his encouragement! Thanks also to Midpoint Trade Books for distributing *Cold Calling for Women*.

I also want to thank Jack Amato, James Benard, Lynda Decker, Terance Rosenthal, Jerry Segal, Mitch Turner and Lance Vernon for taking the time out of their busy lives to help make *Cold Calling for Women* possible. Thanks also to Melissa Wahl, Eunice Salton and Marcia Worthing for their help and advice.

And finally, many, many thanks to anyone and everyone that I ever cold called in my entire life!

Wendy

 # Foreword

Fear of calling prospects can be crippling to new salespeople, and to more than a few experienced ones. I know, because in my own businesses I have hired thousands of women and trained them to sell. The same fear is brought up by members of my audience as I speak to numerous sales groups all over the world.

This magnificent book, *Cold Calling for Women,* is the best I have ever read on this subject. Wendy Weiss has given us a clear, easy-to-understand, logical and inspiring map of exactly how to banish forever the fear of cold calls and instead turn them into big sales.

She teaches us how to put rhythm and tempo into the basic parts of cold calling. I like her practical, down-to-earth style that reminds me of a scout showing the wagon trains the way west. There is not a page here that does not clearly set out the best way to go and how to avoid the hazards so many fear.

I love the way Wendy uses quotations and significant words. You will want to copy them and put them up where you can read them and absorb them. I love one that fits perfectly with her style: it is the word "persuasion," which comes into English from a French root.

"Persuasion means to simply give great and good advice… in advance."

This book is a powerful friend. Open these pages—Wendy Weiss is waiting to show you the way.

Dottie Walters

Dottie Walters is a speaker, consultant, and author of books and audio albums on sales; president of Walters International Speakers Bureau; publisher/editor of *Sharing Ideas Newsmagazine*; and founder of the Speakers Bureau Association and the International Group of Agents & Bureaus (IGAB). She can be reached by phone at (626) 335-8069, and her WebSite is *www.walters-intl.com*.

 # Introduction

Dear Reader:

Welcome to *Cold Calling for Women: Opening Doors & Closing Sales.*

Cold calling is direct, proactive and personal—it allows you to stay in control of the sales process. Rather than waiting for your prospect to come to you, you go directly to your prospect. Prospecting by telephone is convenient—you are in your own space with all of your information at your fingertips; fast—you waste no time traveling, sitting in traffic or office lobbies; and far-reaching—you can contact the largest number of prospects. You can call all over the world! In addition, expenses for this type of new-business development are minimal; you do not have to invest in expensive equipment or new supplies. All you need is a telephone and your leads.

Most people tell me that they hate cold calling and prospecting for new clients or customers. I've heard many reasons and excuses not to cold call: "I'm busy," "It doesn't work," "I prefer referrals," "I don't know what to say," "They just say no…." What is behind this distaste, this fear which cuts across all types of businesses, enterprises and sales? Cold calling can be the great leveler, making everyone equal in avoidance, fear and frustration. But for those of you reading this book, those days are over!

Many people do cold call easily and successfully. They have no fear, or if they do, they've conquered it. They approach cold calling and prospecting with a much different attitude from the above "Telephone Terror." What is this confident attitude? How did they find it? Or are they just "born salespeople?" While it's true that some people are just born with the "gift of gab," given the proper attitude and skills anyone can cold call successfully. And this set of skills and attitudes can be learned.

While this book deals primarily with appointment setting, the techniques work if you are closing on the telephone as well. My intent is to be practical. Therefore, the process I outline in this book is about what works and what does not work. There is no right or wrong here. If you have a technique or system that works for you—keep using it! But if you are not having the success you envision, or if you would like additional techniques to add to your repertoire—this system works!

Now a bit about me. Since 1988 I have been a marketing consultant specializing in new-business development, cold calling and appointment setting. I have represented clients in fields as diverse as the graphic arts to financial services, cold calling and setting appointments for my clients to expand their customer bases. I have made millions and millions of cold calls and have set up hundreds of thousands of new business appointments. I know the cold calling problems, from locating and naming the decision-maker to actually getting the decision-maker on the telephone and having them agree to a meeting. And I have heard just about everything and anything that a prospect might say to a cold caller. In addition I cold call on my own behalf and I have trained salespeople and entrepreneurs in the techniques that I developed over these years. I am also a former ballet dancer and I believe that everything I know in life I learned in ballet class. I use a "performance model" to shape and define how I think about cold calling. This may not make sense to you now, but it will by the time you finish reading this book.

I have titled this book *Cold Calling for Women: Opening Doors & Closing Sales*, and it is based on over 10 years of cold-calling experience. Women frequently have different issues about cold calling and sales than men. How we perceive ourselves, how others perceive us, the societal norms of what is considered to be "feminine" versus the proactive approach needed for sales, all come into play. In *Cold Calling for Women* I address these concerns and I have set out clearly and succinctly the step-by-step what, why and how of cold calling. Whether you are a beginner or a seasoned cold caller looking to improve your skills, if you follow the steps I've laid out, your "hit" rate on cold calls will improve.

Chapter 1 introduces a new way to approach cold calling and *Chapter 2* outlines everything you need to start. *Chapters 3,4* and *5* detail how to develop your strategic marketing plan for cold calling—the What, Who and Where: What are you selling? Who will buy it? Where will you find them? *Chapter 6* outlines the elements of an effective cold-calling script, while *Chapter 7* will ensure that your delivery of that script works. *Chapter 8* focuses on eliminating "Telephone Terror." *Chapter 9* tells you how to put a name on your prospect. *Chapter 10* outlines specific techniques to get past all of the screens and actually get that named prospect on the telephone! In *Chapter 11* you learn how to make sure that once you have the named prospect on the telephone they are indeed the decision-maker. And *Chapter 12* gives you specific answers to many common prospect objections. *Chapter 13* is a compilation of miscellaneous but important information and *Chapter 14* outlines the "Performance Model" for cold calling. *Chapter 15* gives you valuable tips and *Chapter 16* helps you avoid costly mistakes. *Chapter 17* gives you a last-resort option and *Chapter 18* answers the question everyone wants answered: "How many calls will I need to make?" *Chapter 19* explains "The Game—Let's Make an Appointment!" There is a glossary and recommendations for further resources at the end.

This book is a combination of the "practical" and the "philosophical." Some readers may need only the "how to" sections. Others may need the "theory." Many of you will need help in both areas. Feel free to pick and choose, skipping chapters that may not address your needs. Chapters 1, 7, 8 and 14 cover the more "philosophic" or "theoretical" aspects of cold calling. The rest of the chapters are very practical and specific. "Use what you need, leave the rest behind."

I invite my readers to contact me if you have any questions or comments. And please let me know of your successes! My telephone number is: (212) 463-8212, my e-mail address: wendy@wendyweiss.com, my address: c/o D.F.D. Publications, Inc., P.O. Box 20664, London Terrace Station, New York, NY 10011. I look forward to hearing from you.

Sincerely,

Wendy

Chapter 1:
Making Cold Calls

Definitions

Cold call: "A telephone call or visit made to someone who is not known or not expecting the contact, often in order to sell something." (*American Heritage Dictionary of the English Language, Third Edition* ©1996)

Sell: "To persuade (another) to recognize the worth or desirability of…" (*American Heritage Dictionary of the English Language, Third Edition* ©1996)

Cold calling is a way of introducing yourself, your company, your service, and/or your product to others. It is a way of broadening your range of influence, generating interest and bringing new prospects into your market. The cold call is a way of networking, a way of starting new relationships and, most important, a way of developing and expanding your business.

Some people divide calls into cold calls and warm calls, warm calls being when you have some type of introduction to the prospect, whether it is a referral or that you've sent a letter first. In my opinion—if I do not know the prospect, if I have never spoken with this prospect, I consider this to be a cold call. After all, just because one has a referral or has sent a letter does not necessarily guarantee that the prospect will either see you or purchase your product or service. In addition, I do not believe in sending letters or marketing materials before the call. I believe those types of materials should only be sent as follow-up and support for your cold call. Sending material in advance of your cold call does not "warm up" the prospect—it is actually detrimental. It gives your prospect the opportunity to say, "I've got your materials on file—I'll call you if I need you," which means that you will not get in to see that prospect! More on this later!

I actually prefer to think about this type of "cold" prospecting as "making introductory calls." The terms "cold calling" or "cold prospecting" are scary. Instead I prefer to think of introductions. You are calling someone who potentially *needs* you or your product or service. You are introducing yourself, your company and your product or service. From here on, I will refer to introductory calls rather than cold calls.

Looking at the *American Heritage Dictionary of the English Language* definition of "sell" that begins this chapter ("to persuade [another] to recognize *the worth or desirability of…*"), the definition assumes value. It assumes you recognize the value of whatever it is that you are selling. Inherent in the definition is the concept of worth and desirability.

In order to succeed in sales you *must* believe in the "worth or desirability of" your product or service. Before you can ever convince someone else to buy, you must first "buy into" the

8

worth or desirability of that product or service yourself. Belief in your own integrity and the integrity of your product or service is the cornerstone of making introductory calls and indeed of the entire sales process. If you do not have this deep belief in your product or service, then get another product or service to sell.

The term "sales," unfortunately, has come to be viewed with disrespect, conjuring images of untrustworthiness and deviousness. This is a misconception that does a disservice because in order to do their job, most salespeople really do need to believe in their product. They must believe that they have integrity, that their product or service is meaningful and that they are providing a benefit to their customers. If they do not believe those things, they are generally frustrated, unmotivated and not very good introductory callers or salespeople.

Far too often, however, salespeople buy into this self-image of untrustworthiness, placing themselves in their own minds at a disadvantage and on a lower level than their prospect. Before you begin, then, the first thing you need to do is to examine your business, product or service and to examine how you see yourself in relation to your business and to your client or customer.

♦ What is your product or service?

♦ Is it meaningful?

♦ Does it provide a benefit to your client or customer?

♦ Do you believe in the value and benefit of your product or service?

♦ Are you doing the best you know how to insure that your customers get what they need?

♦ Do you see yourself as an expert?

♦ What is your intent toward your customer?

♦ Is your intent to provide the best that you possibly can, or is it to take advantage and put something over?

If your intent is the latter, perhaps a career change is in order. Otherwise you need to recognize that you are a reputable person with integrity, representing a beneficial product or service. You are in fact providing an important product or service to your clients or customers—one that they want.

Frequently salespeople feel that they need their prospect or customer more than the prospect or customer needs them. You should recognize that if your prospect is already using a similar product or service then they need you or someone just like you. That prospect wants the benefit that product or service provides—they are buying it. Therefore, they need you or someone just like you to provide that benefit! In addition, if you have a new product or service that could be of benefit to your customer, something that might save them time or money, and they are not aware of it—you have a moral obligation to tell them! The telephone connects both ways. The truth is that each person on the line has something of benefit to offer and each does need the other.

The keys to introductory calling are the right attitude and good listening skills. By the right attitude I mean *how* you think about your call. The emotional "baggage" you bring along with you influences your attitude, which you then project in your conversation. Your prospect can hear if you feel unsure, afraid or uncomfortable in the same way that you can pick up those uneasy feelings when speaking with someone. On some level you can help create the attitude of the person to whom you are speaking. If your expectation is that your call will be unwelcome, this will make you anxious and tentative. Your prospect will pick up on that and it will be likely to make her less receptive to you. My expectation is that I will be well received, I will speak with someone who is professional and courteous, and we will both get what we want out of the telephone call. That attitude comes through on the telephone—making my prospect more inclined to listen and respond favorably.

The intent of an introductory call is communication—two-way communication. You want your prospect to hear you, and you also want to hear them. You must listen! A later chapter covers active listening—what the prospect says versus what you hear, projection versus reality. But for now the focus is on your intent, which is communication. Communication is aided by a courteous, businesslike, confident and assured attitude. These days, when people can be so rude and unfriendly, you get bonus points for courtesy! Being polite will put you way ahead in the game. The introductory call is step one of the sales process. Your goal on this type of call is generally an appointment, the opportunity to "get your foot in the door." To reach that goal, however, your intent must be communication with your prospect.

Whether you are calling corporations and Fortune 500 companies or small- to mid-sized businesses, these calls can serve to introduce, network, start a business relationship, get information or a referral and of course to "get your foot in the door." The direct contact of a telephone call cuts down on cumbersome paperwork, time-consuming letter writing and expenses. The telephone "cuts right to the chase"; you find the decision-maker and ask for a decision (an appointment) on the spot. When they say "yes," if they need some type of paperwork, marketing materials, samples... you can send them. If they say "no," then they do not need paperwork, marketing materials or samples. This saves an enormous amount of time, not to mention expense. Compare the cost of a printed mailer (design costs, printing, postage...) or a letter-writing campaign (paper costs, postage...) with that of a telephone call.

Compare also the time you will spend to develop each method. Telephone calls are far less time-consuming and achieve greater results. On average, in one hour you can dial the telephone 20 to 30 times and out of that make 4 to 6 completed calls (where you speak directly with the decision-maker). An average for successful "hits" on a completed call is one out of three or four calls. Your hit rate may be lower, it could be higher.

Letters are also extremely passive. If you do not plan to at least call to follow up on the letter you could wait forever. If you are planning a follow-up call, why not just skip the letter and go right to the call? And as mentioned earlier, sending a letter first can actually decrease your chances of making an appointment with your prospect!

People today get a lot of solicitations and junk mail. It is difficult to make your letter stand out from all the others and it is very easy for your prospect to simply throw your letter out, sometimes without even opening it. A well-presented introductory call however does stand out. It is far more difficult to say "no" to a person than to a piece of paper. The key words here are "well-presented." True, your prospect can say "no" and then hang up, but given your good calling technique, the proper attitude and the right "hook" they probably will not. And if you do not know how to make a good telephone pitch, you can learn. Read Chapters 6 and 7!

Summary

☎ Think of this process as making introductory calls. You are calling to introduce yourself, your product or your service

☎ Introductory calling is a way of expanding and developing business

☎ Introductory calling is communication

☎ Introductory calling is proactive, effective and inexpensive

☎ Step 1 is to examine your business, product or service and how you see yourself and your intentions

☎ Recognize that you are a reputable person with integrity, representing a beneficial product or service

☎ Your prospect needs you!

Chapter 2:
Everything You Need to Start

Things You Need

Environment

All you need to make introductory calls is a telephone and your leads. But you must set up a comfortable space in which to work! It should be organized with all of the tools you will need at your fingertips. Your space should be quiet with no disturbances. You need to be able to focus and concentrate. In addition, it is not considered professional to have music blaring or children—or even colleagues—screaming in the background.

You should clear space on your desk so that you can take notes or have your contact-tracking software open so that you can take notes that way. Work with a script in front of you (more on scripts later)—just in case. You are not on a video monitor, and no one can see if you are working with a script so it's a kind of safety net. Have all the information about your prospects together and in one place and make sure that when you are speaking with a prospect you have it all there in front of you.

Wear comfortable clothes. Again, we are not yet at the day where everyone has a video monitor to go with her telephone. Your prospect cannot see you. It does not matter what you are wearing. It does matter that you are comfortable so that you can focus and concentrate. If your business attire is uncomfortable—change clothes! If your shoes are killing you—take them off!!

Telephone

You must have a good telephone. It is a good idea to have a cordless phone (make sure that the reception is good) or to have a long cord on it so that you can move, pace back and forth, hang from the ceiling—whatever. A headset can be very helpful. (For many years I worked with my telephone lodged between my shoulder and my head. This gave me a perpetual crook in the neck and incredible tension in my shoulders and upper back. Finally I purchased a headset. No more neck, back and shoulder strain!) I strongly recommend that you purchase one. In addition, a headset leaves your hands free. It's easier to take notes, access information or gesture (which—even though your prospect cannot see you—makes your conversation more real.) Make sure that your telephone has a clear sound. If you are not sure, use someone else's phone to call yours and have a colleague standing by to answer it. This way you will know for sure. Your telephone should be push-button—why waste time dialing a rotary phone (should you have such a relic)? And it should have a redial button and memory capacity.

Lead-Tracking System

Set up a calendar and always work with it in front of you. I once knew a consultant who used a two-calendar system. One, an "old-fashioned" appointment book and the other, on her computer. She would frequently forget to check both calendars and end up scheduling two meetings at the same time. This does not work. Pick one—go with it.

Set up your system to keep track of *every single lead*. Along with company name, prospect name, address and telephone number, you need to track dates of contact, what was discussed, dates to call back, if marketing materials were sent, which ones, if samples, which ones, etc. You want to make sure that you have the correct spelling of your prospect's name (everyone likes to have their names spelled correctly!) and her full title. And make sure to keep notes of everything. Flag prospects with whom you set up meetings and prospects for follow-up calls. Your system can be as simple as a tickler file or it can be contact-tracking software. Either works. Just make sure you keep track of those leads—it is imperative! One of the biggest mistakes that I made with the dance company that I founded was not keeping good track of leads, contributors and people interested in the group. I duplicated much effort and lost many opportunities—not to mention contributions—this way. Don't make this mistake!

A tickler file is a box with index cards divided by month and date. Get 5"x8" index cards—that way you'll have lots of room to write everything down. Put the company name, address and telephone number along with your prospect's name at the top of the card. Every time you dial the telephone make a note—even if you only reach a voice mail. This way you will have a record of how often you have called and how long it has taken you to reach that particular prospect. This is even more important if a secretary answers the phone. When you are making introductory calls, if a secretary answers the line you should only call that particular prospect a few times on a given day—then you *must stop*! If you call too frequently, you will "blow your cover" (more on this later). So put that number aside until another day and work with other leads. And don't leave messages—no one will ever call you back.

Company Name: ABC Company
Address: 1 Main St.
Telephone Number: 765-4321

Prospect Name: Jane Jones

Date: May 10

When you do reach your prospect keep writing. The more information that you record, the easier your next call will be to that prospect. If another call is necessary you can use that information to refer back to your previous conversation. When you do speak with your prospect, if they tell you to call back on a certain date, simply move their card to that date in the box. If they have requested marketing materials or samples, put those in a separate section (called "Send Literature" or "Send Samples") until they go out. Then move those cards to the appropriate dates for follow up. On any given day you should have brand new leads along with leads previously called but not reached or previously directly contacted.

Company Name: ABC Company
Address: 1 Main St.
Telephone Number: 765-4321

Prospect Name: Jane Jones

Date: May 10

Jane said she is very busy now. Call her in 2 weeks to schedule meeting. In the meantime, send samples.

Date: May 11

Samples go out.

Date: May 24

Meeting schedule: June 26, @ 10:00 a.m. w/ Jane

There are many different types of contact-tracking software on the market. The basic principle, however, is that of the tickler file above. Contact-tracking software does, of course, have many other functions—sending letters, faxes, e-mail, creating calendars… and ultimately you will need to get it—contact-tracking software will make your life and your follow-up much easier! It eliminates a lot of manual labor and saves time. You have to enter information only once—addresses, for example. After that, to do a mailing you can mail merge and print labels without having to again type addresses. You can also pick out specific groups from your database for calls, mailings, broadcast fax or e-mails. Contact-tracking software will even remind you when it is time to make a specific telephone call! You must, however, keep track of all information pertaining to your leads. So if you do not yet have contact-tracking software, use the tickler file—it works—and use it all of the time! If you are using contact-tracking software track the same information that you would with a tickler file and use your contact-tracking software all of the time! This way you'll keep your data up to date and not lose out on any opportunities.

Time

Make time to prospect. Set aside a part of your day for calling and make sure that you *do it*! To be successful, introductory calling needs to be done on a regular basis. Try, however, to vary your calling times—you will be able to reach some prospects at one time of the day and others at other times of the day. It is a good idea to keep notes of your calling times and the time that you reach a particular prospect, especially if they prove difficult to reach. It is a good bet that if you have to call that prospect back you will be able to reach her at around the same time.

Good times for calling senior-level people are generally early mornings before 9:00 A.M. or early evening after 5:00 P.M. Frequently secretaries are gone and prospects will answer their own phones. Lunch is also a good time; again, secretaries might be out and the prospect may be answering her own telephone. You may find that there are good calling times for your particular industry. I once was calling Creative Directors in advertising agencies and found that for the most part, I could not begin to reach them until after 10:00 A.M.—so I would start my calls at 10:00 A.M. But you must make calls. You will not reach any prospects if you do not make calls!

Things to Do

Do your homework. Set up your strategic marketing plan: Define your product or service—features, selling points and customer benefits—and define your customer/client profile. (Some of this will parallel the work you should have already done for your product/service—some, because this is a plan specifically for introductory calling, will differ.) I detail all of this at length in the following chapters.

Next, write your script. When your prospect does pick up the telephone you must be prepared with what you are going to say. Chapter 6 outlines how to write a compelling introductory-calling script. In addition, your script must include answers to the objections you are bound to hear from your prospects. Chapter 12 outlines specific answers to very common objections that prospects voice. Your industry may have additional concerns or objections. You must be prepared with the answers.

Making Telephone Calls

And last, but not least, you will need to make telephone calls. Reading this book and following this advice does not mean that you will never again have to dial the telephone. Instead what it means is that your "hit" rate on an introductory call will go up. Part of sales is simply numbers. By using these methods you will be able to increase the number of times that you can reach your prospect directly, you will make more appointments and get in more doors. But the more numbers you dial the better your success and "hit" rate will be. And the more doors you open, the more sales you will close!

Summary

☎ Set up a comfortable environment in which to work

☎ Get a cordless telephone or one with a long cord, clear sound, push buttons, a redial button and memory capacity. Get a headset!

☎ Set up a system to track all of your leads—and use it all of the time!

☎ Make time to prospect. Keep track of the times that are best to reach your prospects

☎ Do your homework: set up your strategic marketing plan and write your script

☎ Make telephone calls!

Chapter 3:
Why Your Customer or
Client Needs You

You would never dream of attending a meeting with a major client or customer without being prepared. You would want to establish:

♦ Who are you meeting?

♦ What is the agenda?

♦ What does your client or customer need?

♦ What materials and/or information do you need to support your position?

♦ What do you want from the meeting?

Introductory prospecting requires the same type of preparation.

Why Your Customer Needs You

People buy for their own reasons, not for yours. And people buy because they believe that the product or service will get them what they want. And what they really want is a Big Benefit. Big Benefits are things like financial stability, love, recognition, independence... There are many—because they are basic human desires. This section could, from the prospect's point of view, easily be called: "What's in it for me?" Because that is really what your prospect is saying to herself.

A personal example: I enjoy clothes. While I don't really like to shop, I do like to buy. And I am frequently an impulse buyer. I sometimes hear clothes in displays or in stores calling to me: "Buy me! Buy me! Take me home!" Frequently I do. The truth is, however, I'm not buying just the garment, I am buying how the garment makes me feel. When I am well dressed I feel secure, confident, glamorous, fashionable and it's fun! I like the feeling. I buy it often. I am not buying to keep a store in business or help out a designer, I am buying because I want the Big Benefit of feeling fabulous, which I do feel when I'm wearing something I like.

Another example: You have purchased this book. In it I tell you that I have been in business for over 10 years. Now if I were to simply stop there, your response might be—"so what?" And you'd be right! It is my job to point out that those years give me the background to write this book. And in over 10 years of making introductory calls I developed the techniques that I now write about—and these techniques work! You did not buy this book because I have been in business for years, you bought this book so that you could improve your introductory calling skills, so that you could open more doors, thereby closing more sales and thereby *making more money*! The Big Benefit that you seek is *more money*!

Customers and clients want what they want; not what you think they may want or should want. They have their own reasons for buying. You may have to help them identify those reasons, but they will be theirs, not yours.

Step One: Determining Benefits

While your customers will buy for their own reasons, they need you to provide the product or service that will deliver their desired benefits. You are the link between their desire and its fulfillment. That is why I call this chapter *"Why Your Customer Needs You."* Your customer has the need, the desire, and the want. You have the product or service that will give your prospects the benefit they seek. Eureka!

The first part of determining *Why Your Customer Needs You* is to define your product or service.

♦ What exactly is your product or service?

♦ What exactly does it do?

♦ What purpose does it serve?

Start by listing product/service features. These are things that are facts, they are innate—they are just there. Your product may be a certain size or a certain color. It has a specific price. It may have a specific function. These are facts; they just are.

What you ultimately want to achieve with this exercise is to establish your Customer Benefits. Benefits are what your customer or prospect wants, what will fulfill their needs. What is the benefit that they are seeking that you and your product or service will provide? Many times people confuse features with benefits. Make no mistake; your customer is buying benefits. No matter how fond you may be of these particular product/service features your customer will not care unless they can see the benefit to themselves—that is the "what's in it for me" from your prospect's point of view.

To understand what those benefits are and to clearly define them, start by listing product/service features. This exercise is for you as well as for your customer or prospect. Once you list your product/service features you will be on your way to defining the benefits. Once you have a clear understanding of all of the Customer Benefits and Big Benefits, you will be able to articulate those Benefits to your prospects and your commitment to and belief in your product or service can only deepen.

Let's start with an example of a client who has a video production house and who produces corporate videos. She has been in business for 12 years, has a background in the fine arts and her client base consists primarily of major corporations and Fortune 500 companies. These last three are all features. So this client would fill out the features column as follows:

Features:

1. In business for 12 years
2. Background in the fine arts
3. Customers are major corporations and Fortune 500 companies

Now it is your turn! List the features of your product or service.

Product/Service Features:

1.

2.

3.

4.

5.

6.

7.

8.

9.

10.

Did you do some writing? If you didn't go back and do it now!

Step Two: Defining Selling Points

The next step is to look at these product/service features and define their selling points. A selling point is information about your product or service that is of interest to and will help "sell" your prospect on your product or service. A selling point however, is still not a customer benefit. Your customer will not buy because of a selling point. It is, however, part of defining and pinpointing potential customer benefits and is thus on the path to help your client or customer see the benefit. For example: Your product is a certain size. The selling point for that feature might be that it would then fit in a specific place. But that is not yet the benefit. The benefit might be that because the product fits in a specific place it saves room thereby making possible other uses for the saved space. So potentially the Big Benefit here is efficiency. Because of the size of your product (feature) it fits in a certain space (selling point) which saves room (benefit) which makes possible other uses for that space, creating efficient use of space (Big Benefit). In this scenario, you are selling efficiency.

Your prospects must be drawn clearly and purposefully along the path to the Customer Benefit and Big Benefit. You cannot simply point out a product or service feature or selling point and then expect them to make the connection themselves. You must be the guide.

Using the video production house client again as an example, she defined three features for her product: 1) she's been in business for 12 years, 2) she has a background in the fine arts, 3) her customers are major corporations and Fortune 500 companies. Let's define the selling points:

Selling points:

1. Feature: *In business for 12 years*

   Selling Point: *She has experience*

2. Feature: *She has a background in the arts*

   Selling Point: *She has the appropriate knowledge and skills*

3. Feature: *Customers are major corporations and Fortune 500 companies*

   Selling Point: (Assuming the prospect is another major corporation...) *She works with similar types of businesses and understands their issues, their type of work and their problems*

So now it's your turn. Take each of your product/service features and define their selling points.

List at least one selling point for each product/service feature:

1. Feature:

   Selling Point:

2. Feature:

   Selling Point:

3. Feature:

    Selling Point:

4. Feature:

    Selling Point:

5. Feature:

    Selling Point:

6. Feature:

    Selling Point:

7. Feature:

    Selling Point:

8. Feature:

   Selling Point:

9. Feature:

   Selling Point:

10. Feature:

    Selling Point:

Did you do some writing? If you didn't go back and do it now!

Step Three: Convey Benefit to Prospect

The last step in defining *Why Your Customer Needs You* is to describe clearly and precisely the benefit to your prospect. The preceding two steps should help you achieve this goal.

I worked recently with a graphic designer who wanted to expand her client base. This designer worked mainly in corporations dealing with senior people and working on projects such as annual reports, identity materials and marketing materials. In going through the steps of identifying first the features of her service, then the selling points, benefits and Big Benefits she realized that she was not just selling graphic design services. She was selling Job Security. She was selling job security because these types of projects can frequently make or break an individual's or a company's reputation. Her focus had to be to show her prospect not only that she could do the work (a given) but that everything would turn out well and that her prospect would end up looking good.

Remember that your priorities and needs and those of your prospect do not necessarily coincide. You must be able to point out to your prospect exactly why they should buy from you. This process is not about you—it is about your prospect and what she wants. Your product, for example, may be green—but unless a green product will benefit your prospect in some way, chances are she will not buy it. And it will not matter that you love green! In addition, do not assume that your prospect will be able to guess the product benefits once you list the features or selling points. It is your job to make these benefits clear—and they must be benefits that your prospect *wants*. People buy what they want, not what they need. It does no good to talk of customer benefits that do not interest your prospect—no matter how taken with them you may be. For example, if your prospect has indicated an interest in turnaround time, focus on turnaround time and not on the quality of your product or service! It does not matter how impressed you are with the quality of your product if that is not what interests your potential customer. Remember this is not about you.

When the video producer looked at her selling points these are the benefits she came up with:

Customer Benefits:

1. Feature: *In business for 12 years*

   Selling Point: *She has experience*

   Benefit: *The job will be done right*

2. Feature: *She has a background in the arts*

   Selling Point: *She has the appropriate knowledge and skills*

   Benefit: *The job will be done right*

3. Feature: *Customers are major corporations and Fortune 500 companies*

   Selling Point: (Assuming the prospect is another major corporation...) *She works with similar types of businesses and understands their issues, their type of work and their problems*

   Benefit: *She knows what needs to be done. She can give advice and avoid costly errors. The job will be done right the first time*

Now it's your turn. List the customer benefits of your product or service. For each selling point that you previously listed define a customer benefit. If you cannot define a benefit—leave it out!

List at least one Customer Benefit for each Selling Point:

1. Selling point:

    Benefit:

2. Selling point:

    Benefit:

3. Selling point:

    Benefit:

4. Selling point

    Benefit

5. Selling point:

    Benefit:

6. Selling point:

   Benefit:

7. Selling point:

   Benefit:

8. Selling point:

   Benefit:

9. Selling point:

   Benefit:

10. Selling point:

    Benefit:

Did you do some writing? If you didn't go back and do it now!

Now from Customer Benefits to Big Benefits. For the video producer as follows:

Big Benefits:

1. Feature: *In business for 12 years*
   Selling Point: *She has experience*
   Benefit: *The job will be done right*
   Big Benefit: *Ease of mind/Cost savings…*

2. Feature: *She has a background in the arts*
   Selling Point: *She has the appropriate knowledge and skills*
   Benefit: *The job will be done right*
   Big Benefit: *Ease of mind/Cost savings…*

3. Feature: *Customers are major corporations and Fortune 500 companies*
   Selling Point: (If the prospect is a major corporation…) *She works with similar types of businesses and understands their issues, their type of work and their problems*
   Benefit: *She knows what needs to be done. She can give advice and avoid costly errors. The job will be done right the first time*
   Big Benefit: *Ease of mind/Cost savings…*

Now it's your turn. Look at your Customer Benefits and take the time to identify the Big Benefit for each:

List one Big Benefit for each Customer Benefit:

1. Customer Benefit:

   Big Benefit:

2. Customer Benefit:

   Big Benefit:

3. Customer Benefit:

   Big Benefit:

4. Customer Benefit:

   Big Benefit:

5. Customer Benefit:

   Big Benefit:

6. Customer Benefit:

   Big Benefit:

7. Customer Benefit:

Big Benefit

8. Customer Benefit

Big Benefit:

9. Customer Benefit:

Big Benefit:

10. Customer Benefit:

Big Benefit:

Did you do some writing? If you didn't go back and do it now!

If you have done these exercises, you now have solid reasons that a potential customer needs you and should purchase your product or service. And always remember: *It's the Benefits!*

Summary

☎ People buy for their own reasons—i.e. It's the Benefits!

☎ Start by defining product or service features, things that are just there

☎ Next define your product or service selling points, this is step two in the process of defining benefits

☎ Then define your Customer Benefits—the "what's in it for me?" from your prospect or customer's point of view

☎ Finally, identify the Big Benefits—financial stability, love, recognition, ease of mind, independence.... These are basic human desires

☎ It's the Benefits!

Chapter 4:
Who Will Buy Your Wares?

Part of sales is simply numbers. If you were to open the telephone book at random and simply start dialing, and if you kept at it long enough, eventually you would reach someone who was willing to either meet with you or purchase your product or service. But this would neither be fun nor productive. It is a much better idea to contact only those prospects that you think may be viable prospects. To separate viable prospects from all of the others start by developing a Customer Profile. If you've been in business for a while, this is of course easier. You can take a look at your current customer base and assume that similar businesses might be in need of your product or service. Start out with another top-ten list:

List your top ten customers

1. Company name:

   Type of business:

   Title of decision-maker:

2. Company name:
   Type of business:
   Title of decision-maker:

3. Company name:
   Type of business:
   Title of decision-maker:

4. Company name:
   Type of business:
   Title of decision-maker:

5. Company name:
   Type of business:
   Title of decision-maker:

6. Company name:
   Type of business:
   Title of decision-maker:

7. Company name:
   Type of business:
   Title of decision-maker:

8. Company name:

   Type of business:

   Title of decision-maker:

9. Company name:

   Type of business:

   Title of decision-maker:

10. Company name:

    Type of business:

    Title of decision-maker:

Did you do some writing? If you didn't go back and do it now!

Look at what these top ten customers have in common. Is there a similarity in the type of business? Do you find you do most of your business with this type of company? Well, there's your market. What are the titles of the decision-makers, the people who actually buy your product or service? Are they similar? If you find that your customer is generally a widget company and the Director of Thingamajigs or the Senior Vice President of Thingamajigs is usually the title of the decision-maker, then it's a good bet when you go to other widget companies the title of the decision-maker will be something like Director of Thingamajigs or Senior Vice President of Thingamajigs. When you are making introductory calls and trying to name your prospect, find out who is the Director or Senior Vice President of Thingamajigs and that is probably the name of the person with whom you need to speak. If it is not, that person can probably give you the correct name.

A more concrete example: over the years several of my clients have been graphic-design firms. One of my clients was particularly interested in going to advertising agencies. We found that the decision-maker for hiring graphic artists at advertising agencies is generally the Creative Director, or Senior Vice President/Creative Director. Sometimes it was someone in Production, a Production Director, Production Manager, sometimes an Art Buyer, sometimes an Art Director. Sometimes there were several independent decision-makers and I would try to set my client up with all of them. I knew, however, that if I called an advertising agency and asked for the Creative Director... or one of those other titles, I would probably be in the right area. Then I would try to reach the highest-level person I could find in that area. If that person was not the decision-maker they could tell me who was. In addition, the prospect to whom they directed me usually reported to them or reported to someone who reported to them. So I could call the newly named prospect and say, "Jane Jones (subtext: your boss) said..."

There may be other similarities in your customer base, for example, demographics or geographic location, number of employees or type of equipment used. Take the time to fully break down all of the similarities in your customer base. The more clearly you can define your potential customer the easier it will be to find them.

If you've been in business for a while it is also a good idea to look at your historical customer. Is the type of customer you used to do business with different from your current customer? How? And why? Has the market changed or is this just a large market segment you've forgotten about? If the market has not changed significantly, go back and analyze your historic customers in the same manner that you analyzed your current customers. Establish, as you did with current customers, the type of business and usual title of the decision-maker. Then your call is to either reconnect with, or find new prospects in those market areas.

Another good place to look is at your competition. If you have not been in business too long or are just starting out you can actually begin with this. Who are your competition's customers? They are your potential customers as well. You may need some subterfuge here, but call your competition and ask for their marketing materials. If need be, act like a potential customer, or if you feel uncomfortable doing this get a friend to do it for you. Generally, marketing materials will list past and/or current customers. You can analyze these in the same manner that you analyzed your current customers. What types of businesses are these? Who are the decision-makers? With that list of your competition's customers you will also have a list of qualified prospects for your own product or service!

The idea in creating your customer profile is to focus and target your best prospects. You may find that you have several markets or categories of prospects. Your customer profiles for each of these categories may differ. By breaking down each category as specifically as you can you will increase your ability to target and locate your most viable prospects.

Look also at your list of selling points and benefits. Knowing the benefit of your product/service will frequently lead you directly to whomever it is who needs that particular benefit. Suppose you are in the insurance industry. A Big Benefit you may be selling is "security," that if your client has a problem, they will still be okay. Look at who might be at risk. Now here your answer may be, "everyone is at risk, everyone needs security." And that is true. If, however, you are selling auto insurance, people without cars would not be in the "at risk" category. You want to stay away from thinking that "everybody" needs your product or service and instead target those who specifically need your product or service.

Customer Profile

	Top 10	**Historical**	**Competition**
Type of business:			
Title of decision-maker:			
Similarities:			

The final part of your customer profile is to decide what are your qualifying parameters—the conditions that are necessary for you to consider doing business with this prospect. These qualifying parameters will depend on your product or service. Possibly the prospect company should have profits in excess of a particular dollar amount, possibly they need to have a specific number of employees, perhaps they must be located in a specific geographic region… And your qualifying criteria may be different in your different categories. Once you have done your customer profile, you will be able to establish these Qualifying Parameters. Using the car insurance example above, one Qualifying Parameter would be that the prospect must own a car!

Going back to the video producer example from previous chapters, some of her qualifying parameters are:

Qualifying Parameters:

1. The prospect company does not have in-house video production facilities.
2. The prospect company has an adequate budget for video.
3. The prospect company produces at least one video per year.

Now it's your turn! Establish your Qualifying Parameters:

Qualifying Parameters:

1.

2.

3.

4.

5.

6.

7.

8.

9.

10.

Did you do some writing? If you didn't go back and do it now!

Once you know your qualifying parameters it is not difficult to find the information to qualify your prospect companies. Many directories, besides listing names and telephone numbers, give all sorts of additional valuable information about their listings (i.e., products, customers, profits, losses...) The worst-case scenario is to simply ask your prospect directly.

In addition to your qualifying parameters, you need to establish qualifying questions for your specific prospects. These are predetermined questions which when asked of your prospect help to determine whether or not they are a viable potential customer and also whether or not they are the decision-maker. Qualifying questions can be: "What is your budget for this type of project?" "Who is your current vendor?" "How often do you purchase...?" "Who else is involved in this decision?" You need to pinpoint exactly what it is that you need to know in order to determine the quality of a particular lead and to establish whether it is worth your time and energy to go after this lead. And again, qualifying questions may be different if you have different target categories with different qualifying parameters. That is why you listed Qualifying Parameters. Now, take your qualifying parameters and turn them into Qualifying Questions for your prospect.

For the video producer, her qualifying parameters turned into these qualifying questions:

1. *Qualifying Parameter*: The prospect company does not have in-house video production facilities and/or does work with outside video production facilities.

   Qualifying Question: "How did you produce your last video?"

49

2. *Qualifying Parameter*: The prospect company has an adequate budget for video.

   Qualifying Question: "On average... what is your budget for this type of project?" (Prospects sometimes do not want to discuss dollar amounts or budgets on the telephone. That is why it is a good idea to use phrases like "on average" or "ballpark figure..." These phrases are less scary to your prospect.)

3. *Qualifying Parameter*: The prospect company produces at least one video per year.

   Qualifying Question: "On average... how many videos do you produce in a year?" (Again, sometimes prospects do not like to get too specific. Phrases like "on average" or "generally" take the pressure off your prospect so that they do not feel they are revealing too much.)

Now it's your turn! List your Qualifying Questions below:

Qualifying Questions:

1.

2.

3.

4.

5.

6.

7.

8.

9.

10.

Did you do some writing? If you didn't go back and do it now!

Summary

☎ Start by listing your top ten customers along with the type of business, title of the decision-maker and any other similarities you notice

☎ Analyze your historical customers in the same manner you just analyzed your top ten customers

☎ Analyze your competition's customers—they are your potential customers as well

☎ Product/service benefits can lead you to whomever it is who needs that particular benefit

☎ List your Qualifying Parameters—the conditions that are necessary for you to consider doing business with a prospect

☎ Turn your Qualifying Parameters into Qualifying Questions for your prospect

☎ Chapter 5:
Where Will You Find Your Client or Customer?

At this point you should have established who is your potential client or customer. You know what types of businesses may need your product or service and the titles of those within the prospect companies who may actually be the decision-makers on the purchase of your product or service. You have also established a list of strong customer benefits—reasons that your potential customer should buy from you—and you have your qualifying criteria and questions. You are all set. You just need to find your prospects. To do that, put together a list of potential leads for your introductory calling campaign. You need specific company names, telephone numbers and prospect names. Where do you look for this?

Go to the library. There are trade directories, association directories, industry directories... Take a look at:

Directories in Print and
Encyclopedia of Business & Professional Associations
The Gale Group
27500 Drake Rd.
Farmington Hills, MI 48331-3535
(248) 699-GALE (tel.)
(800) 877-GALE (toll-free)
(800) 414-5043 (fax)
Internet: http://www.gale.com

National Trade and Professional Associations
    of the United States and
State and Regional Associations of the United States
Columbia Books, Inc.
1825 Connecticut Ave., N.W.
Suite 625
Washington, DC 20009
(202) 464-1662 (tel.)
(202) 464-1775 (fax)
Internet: http://www.columbiabooks.com

Associations Yellow Book
Leadership Directories Inc.
104 5th Ave.
New York, NY 10011
(212) 627-4140 (tel.)
(212) 645-0931 (fax)
or

1001 G Street, N.W.
Washington, DC 20004
(202) 347-7757 (tel.)
(202) 628-3430 (fax)
Internet: http://www.leadershipdirectories.com

National Directory of Woman-Owned Business Firms and
Regional Directory of Minority- and Woman-Owned
    Business Firms (Eastern, Central, Western)
Business Research Services, Inc.
4201 Connecticut Ave., N.W.
Suite 610
Washington, DC 20008
(202) 364-6473 (tel.)
(800) 845-8420 (toll-free)
(202) 686-3228 (fax)
email: brspubs@sba8a.com

These books will give you an idea what may be available.
There are many more resources at the library. You can also
call trade journals in your field to see if they publish
directories; your local chamber of commerce probably has a
directory; and of course don't forget any organizations or
associations that you belong to—they probably have
membership directories as well.

I have also had great success, especially for my dance
company, calling from the Yellow Pages. I once found one of
our finest board members (by accident) in the telephone
book. My dance company was producing a benefit and we
wanted to serve wine to our guests. From the Yellow Pages I
called a wine-importing company to solicit a donation. The

55

contact at the wine importers was extremely friendly and quite interested in our work. She did donate the wine; she also attended the benefit, liked what she saw, made a contribution and soon after joined our Board of Directors. She was a powerful and effective board member, handling all of our public relations efforts for several years. We are still friends and get together frequently for dinner. With one telephone call I not only got the needed donation of wine but also a cash contribution and an important addition to our Board of Directors—not to mention a friend!

There are also Yellow Pages on the Internet. Try: USA.com, Yahoo.com, yp.Ameritech.com or do a search for other Yellow Page sites. Once you are at a Yellow Page Web site you can search by business category, business name, location or any criterion you choose.

Additional sources you might contact are:

Standard & Poor's
Money Market Directories, Inc.
320 East Main Street
Charlottesville, VA 22902
(434) 977-1450 (tel.)
(800) 446-2810 (toll-free)
(434) 971-8738 (fax)
Internet: http://www.mmdaccess.com

Standard & Poor's
55 Water Street
New York, NY 10041
(212) 438-1000 (tel.)
Internet: http://www.standardandpoors.com\ratings

Dalton Directory
410 Lancaster Avenue
Haverford, PA 19041
(610) 649-2680 (tel.)
(800) 221-1050 (toll-free)
(610) 649-3596 (fax)
Internet: http://www.daltondirectory.com

Dun & Bradstreet
3 Sylvan Way
Parsippany, NJ 07054
(973) 605-6000 (tel.)
(800) 526-0651 (toll-free)
Internet: http://www.dnb.com

O'Dwyer's Directories
J. R. O'Dwyer Co. Inc.
271 Madison Avenue
New York, NY 10016
(212) 679-2471 (tel.)
(212) 683-2750 (fax)
Internet: http://www.odwyerpr.com

Lists are everywhere. All you really need to begin is the company name and the main telephone number. Everything else—name of decision-maker, correct company address, etc.—you can find out in your telephone call.

As a last resort you can always rent a list. I have not been a big fan of marketed lists since early in my introductory-calling career. One of my first clients was a marketing consultant and a large part of her business was list rental. She hired me to make introductory calls and to help develop her business. Our deal almost fell through when at first she did not want to part with one of her lists so I could begin my calling. She felt her lists were top secret and she had a difficult time in deciding whether or not to give me top-secret security clearance. We were at a standstill. Finally she made the decision to give clearance and I began making calls. Unfortunately I soon found out that most of the people on these top-secret lists were either no longer employed at those companies, hadn't been there for years or else were dead. I soon stopped asking for the individuals listed, and just called the company switchboard and got the name on my own. It was faster and simpler.

No doubt there are lists on the market that are better than the ones compiled by my erstwhile client, but in general I prefer to research a name on my own. This way I know for sure that the prospects are alive and working at the targeted companies. It is a little more time-consuming but worth it. (If you do ask for an individual who is no longer with the company, find out who has taken over for that person. Simply ask: "Who has taken over for her?" You can also find out where the original prospect went. Ask: "Where did Jane Jones go?" This gives you two potential leads.) A note here: I am not talking about direct-mail lists—that is an entirely different subject. And by the way, if you are doing direct mail it is possible to go to a service bureau and get telephone numbers to go with those addresses. Your list broker can make recommendations.

If you are going to rent a list find a broker with whom you are comfortable—someone who listens to your needs, is knowledgeable and helpful. And be as specific as you can be about your parameters. The list broker acts as a liaison between you and the list owner. The broker works for you. Other places to find lists are from list owners, i.e. companies or organizations that own their own in-house lists and rent them out, or from list managers who are hired by list owners to manage and market their lists. Lists are generally rented on a one-time basis. If you rent a list and turn a prospect into a client that client then becomes part of your in-house list or database (which you can later rent out!).

Hot Leads

Finally, once you have all of these company names and all of these telephone numbers, how do you sort them out and determine which exactly is a *hot* lead? If you have carefully done your strategic marketing plan and your customer profile the *hot* leads should be fairly apparent. Which companies fit your ideal customer profile? Those are your *hot* leads.

I recommend dividing your leads into A, B and C lists according to the priority you give them—A being high priority and C the lowest priority. You can move leads from list to list as you gather new information. This way you can concentrate on the leads that have the most potential. I do suggest, however, that if you are a beginner, or just not yet comfortable with your introductory-calling skills, start with your C list. It will be low priority, low anxiety, you will get some practice and you will schedule some new business meetings in the process!

Summary

☎ Go to the library. Look at:

- ◆ *Directories in Print*
- ◆ *Encyclopedia of Business and Professional Associations*
- ◆ *National Trade and Professional Associations of the United States*
- ◆ *State and Regional Associations of the United States*
- ◆ *Associations Yellow Book*
- ◆ *National Directory of Woman-Owned Business Firms*
- ◆ *Regional Directory of Minority- and Woman-Owned Business Firms*

☎ Additional resources:

- ◆ Standard & Poor's
- ◆ *Dalton Directories*
- ◆ Dun & Bradstreet
- ◆ *O'Dwyer's Directories*
- ◆ The Telephone Book
- ◆ Internet Yellow Pages

☎ You can also rent lists

☎ How to determine a hot lead?—Do your homework!

Chapter 6:
When They Say "Hello," What Do You Say?

Many people think they can just "wing it" or they "know what they want to say." On the telephone, however, you have 10 seconds to grab and hold your prospect's attention and frequently you don't get a second chance. Ten seconds goes by very quickly. Your first impression has to be strong enough to carry you through the rest of your pitch. "Winging it" is risky and just generally doesn't work, and "knowing what you want to say" without having actually crafted your message and practiced it can easily turn into "gee, I didn't say that very well...." In addition, when you have to think about what you are going to say it is extremely difficult to focus on and listen to your prospect. You will be nervous and anxious and thinking about what might happen rather than focusing on what is happening.

Like the Girl Scouts, it is better to be prepared. A good script, a well-thought-out presentation that says what you want to say, precisely and succinctly, yet that still gives you room to maneuver, is one of the keys to a successful telephone pitch. This is about communication and about being prepared. In writing your script you are crafting a message and focusing your message to your prospect. Your goal with your script is for your prospect to hear you and for your prospect to get "hooked."

So what makes a good script? Write your script the way you talk—and get to the point! Written language and spoken language are very different. If your script is in written language you will sound phony. Real people do not speak with capital letters at the start of sentences and periods at the end. People actually speak more in phrases or fragments, with pauses, sometimes improper grammar and the occasional "ah" or "um...." It is imperative that you sound real, so if you are having a difficult time with this, try talking into a tape recorder, then playing it back and writing down what you say.

Don't bother asking your prospect "how are you today?" or "may I have a moment of your time?" or anything else. Start by asking for your prospect by name. You have probably already asked the secretary for your prospect by name but when you think your prospect is on the line, ask again. "Jane Jones please." There are two good reasons to do this. Reason number one—everyone loves the sound of their own name, and reason number two—the more practical reason—you want to make sure that it is indeed your prospect on the other end of the line and not the secretary or someone who picked up by mistake. Then greet your prospect, "Hello Jane" or "Hello Ms. Jones"—whichever way you are comfortable. Next, introduce yourself. "My name is (*your name goes here*), my company is (*your company name goes here*)" or "My name is (*your name goes here*), I'm with (*your company name goes here*)."

Then your sound bite. A sound bite is one sentence, which expresses simply and succinctly what you do (or what is your product or service). Example: Wendy Weiss teaches people to get what they want over the telephone.

So in one sentence you must describe what you or your company do. If you do not have a good, solid sound-bite description, stop here and work on it till you do.

My Sound Bite:

Did you do some writing? If you didn't go back and do it now!

Your sound bite, or the following line, should position you as the expert—someone (company, product or service) who stands out from the pack. If you do this well you will preempt the objection: "I can't meet with every salesperson who calls." You will not be "every salesperson who calls." To do this, you cannot say the same things that everyone else is saying—so be creative! When I started my business there were many others providing similar services representing companies, making calls and setting new business appointments for sales representatives. Generally these people worked in-house, were not particularly well paid and were called telemarketers. Even this early in my career I knew

I was not a telemarketer. I decided I was a *Marketing Consultant Specializing in New Business Development*. This put me in a different category altogether. I was the expert, the outside consultant hired to help develop new business. I could set my own fees and work the way I wanted to work and build my business.

Another example: I have a client with whom I work setting up new business meetings. He is a printer—and New York City is full of printers! So this is how I position my client and myself as experts. After introducing myself and my client and giving my one sentence sound bite, I say: "…we're educated, we're accommodating and we're reasonable people!" At this point my prospect and I are no longer talking about printing—we are talking about people! I have changed the subject, taking my client out of the "printer" category and placing him in the "people" category. This sentence does something else—it positions me, my client and the company on the same side as our prospect, with all of the uneducated, unaccommodating, unreasonable printers on the other side! Since anyone who has had any printing done has probably had at least one bad experience, they identify with this sentence and I have them hooked. The last thing this particular sentence does is to make the prospect laugh. Laughter is a great connecting force. I have included the text of my appointment-setting script for this client at the end of the chapter.

Find a way to set yourself up as the expert. You can use phrases like "we specialize in…" or "our reputation is…" "we are known for…." You can also name-drop credentials to help this positioning. Mention clients or customers in similar businesses as your prospect. This does two things: it lets your prospect know that you are familiar with their industry and it will also make prospects feel safer if they have not heard of you before. Most people do not like being trailblazers and instead prefer to follow another's lead. If they know that you work with others in their field they are more inclined to pay attention. Do try and sound bored when you name-drop credentials. It's reverse psychology; if you sound impressed with your client list, you can also sound rather foolish. If, however, you sound unimpressed with your client list, it is actually a strong way of positioning yourself as the expert. In addition, if someone has referred you, this is a good place to drop his or her name. Take the time now to position yourself and/or your company as the expert.

I am the Expert!:

Credentials

Our reputation is… We are known for…

I've been referred by…

Did you do some writing? If you didn't go back and do it now!

Next is the heart of the script. Describe your product or service, pointing out relevant customer benefits. Remember— your customers are interested in benefits, not features and not even selling points. Since you have already done your strategic marketing plan for introductory calling and identified Customer Benefits and Big Benefits in Chapter 3, this is easy. In addition, when you point out the relevant customer benefits remember, as much as possible with the limited knowledge you may initially have of your prospect, to point out customer benefits that may actually interest your prospect. Your prospect will buy for her reasons, not yours. That is why it is important to do your research so that you have a sense of what your prospect may need and may be interested in.

Focus your message to your prospect and speak in their language. If your industry has a particular jargon—don't they all?—use it. You cannot be the expert if you do not know the language. If, however, you are in an industry that has a jargon—but your prospect doesn't know or use that jargon— speak plainly! Your intent here is communication. You want to be understood! This part of your script does not need to be long and unwieldy—a few salient points will do. You can bolster this section with a success story, something you, your company or product did for a customer. How you saved them money, or saved them time or saved the day when they were in a tight spot. By inference, this will mean that you will do the same for your prospect. It is also a way of pointing out customer benefits without actually having to say "and the benefit to you, Ms. Prospect, is…" You might have several different success stories that you use depending on the type of lead on which you are working.

I recently worked with an accountant who is starting his own business. This client had no background in sales and had absolutely no idea about how to even begin to make introductory calls. He came up with several different success stories about clients in different industries and how he saved them money. He then targeted these stories to the appropriate prospects. He had a success story about an entrepreneur starting a new business—he told this to other entrepreneurs starting new businesses.... He had a success story about an attorney—he used this success story with other attorneys.... These stories showed by inference that he understood their businesses, their needs and their problems. He had helped others with exactly the same businesses, needs or problems— he could therefore help his prospect as well. You can use success stories in exactly the same manner.

Your script is fluid. How your conversation with your prospect proceeds will determine what parts of your script you will use. So make sure to leave some maneuvering room in your script so that if you need to change tactics, for example tell a different success story, you can easily do it. You make sure that you have maneuvering room by being prepared, knowing your selling points and customer benefits and knowing which selling points and benefits may interest a particular prospect. Also have several success stories that you can use depending on the point you are trying to make. And please, don't be afraid to say the unexpected or to use humor. Yes, this is business, but we don't have to be dull about it.

Customer Benefits:

Success Stories:

1.

2.

3.

4.

Did you do some writing? If you didn't go back and do it now!

Then the close. Here it is... *Ask for what you want!* All your hard work is worth nothing if you do not *ask for what you want.* Do not expect that your prospect will know what you want, or guess what you want, or offer what you want... It is your job to ask, clearly and precisely.

So, what do you want? You have done your marketing plan; you have defined your potential prospect, type of business, probable title of decision-maker.... But what exactly do you want from that decision-maker? Most would probably answer that you want to turn your prospect into your customer. You want your prospect to buy your product or service. That's all true, but that comes later. What you want now is to get your "foot in the door." You want to introduce yourself, your product and/or your company so that later the prospect can be induced to buy. If your prospect does not know you, is not familiar with your product or service, they will never buy it. They have to know you exist before they will even consider making that purchase! Therefore what you want *now* is an appointment. At this moment you are not selling your product or your service, you are selling an appointment and *only an appointment*. You want the prospect to give you 10 to 15 minutes of their time, so that you can introduce yourself, your company, your product, your service—that is it! At this point you are not asking the prospect to do anything but give you time. You are not asking her to buy anything or change anything that she does—only to meet with you.

If you think about the appointment in this manner, you will also realize that almost any objection to a meeting that your prospect may voice is then largely irrelevant. Perhaps your prospect already has a vendor that provides a similar product or service. So what. None of us can predict the future. The situation could change. Besides, you're not asking that she buy anything, you want to meet with her and introduce yourself. Period! Perhaps your prospect doesn't use a similar product or service and says she has no need. She doesn't need it; she will never need it. So what. None of us can predict the future, anything is possible, and one day perhaps she may.

Now I am not suggesting that you spend your time setting up meetings with people who do not need your product or service, but what I am saying is that the qualification is on *your* part, you actually need to decide if *you* want to meet *this* prospect. Is this prospect worth *your* time and energy?

Salespeople frequently ask me about closing a sale. Closing a sale is certainly your ultimate goal. You will also use many of the same techniques to close that you use in introductory calling. At this moment, however, your focus must be on "getting in the door." This is step one and all of the other steps follow this. You cannot allow your anxiety about closing a sale to interfere with the step you need to start the process that ultimately will effect that sale.

When making introductory calls it is always vital to stay "in the moment." That means that you are only thinking about what you are doing right then. You are not looking at the past; you are not looking into the future. You are in the present—moment by moment. If your previous call was a disaster—it doesn't matter. It is now history. Your focus is on now. When in the middle of an introductory call, you must also be careful not to allow yourself to worry about your future introductory calls. That's in the future. Your focus needs to be totally on what you are doing at the moment. And what you should be doing at the moment is making an appointment.

So with that out of the way—what do you say?

Ask for an appointment—ask for a meeting. I generally like the word "meeting" better than "appointment." It has more weight and substance. Say: "I would like to meet with you," "I would like to introduce myself, my company, my product..." "I need 10 minutes of your time." Be clear, be bold, be to the point. Give them some choices of times: "Is this Thursday good or would next Thursday be better?" It is easier for your prospect to choose between options, such as different dates, than to decide whether and if to schedule. Assume your prospect will schedule the meeting. It makes sense that they would want to. If they are using a similar product or service then they do need you or someone just like you. If you are introducing a product or service that is new or that your prospect is not aware of, something that might save them time or money... as mentioned earlier you have a moral obligation to let them know about it—and they will want to know! Your prospect needs you as much as you need your prospect! After all, it could save them time or money! And it would be very shortsighted on the part of your prospect not to even consider the possibility that their situation could change or that they might find something better than what they now have.

Additionally, if your prospect is already using a similar product or service then making the decision to purchase this particular item is part of their job! And they are supposed to do their job to the best of their ability. Part of that would be finding the best for the least, staying on top of new developments in the field, exploring options, contingency planning... This is where you come in! Meeting with you works to your prospect's advantage. By introducing yourself and your product or service you are helping your prospect to do her job! And what is the Big Benefit? Money. In order to keep a job your prospect needs to do it well. You are a part of that!

The Close:

"I would like to meet with you…"

"I would like to introduce myself, my company, my product…"

"I need 10 minutes of your time."

"Is this Thursday good or would next Thursday be better?"

Your script, however, is not yet done. You also need to have scripted answers to the objections you are bound to hear from any potential prospect. The common ones are: "I'm too busy…" "Send literature/letter/proposal…" "Call me back…" and my favorite: "I don't make appointments…" Possibly there are additional objections that are specific to your industry. You need to be ready.

Given the proper attitude you can view most objections as fairly irrelevant to your goal. *Objections are, however, important clues to what makes your prospect tick.* You must hear your prospect's objections and you must be able to answer them. But if you are totally committed to the idea of scheduling a meeting—and only a meeting—it is easier to come up with answers. Focus on that meeting. Ask for the meeting and keep asking for the meeting. Many common objections are easily answered, and Chapter 12 discusses specific answers for many common objections, but the point here is that you need well-thought-out responses to prospect objections and you must keep your focus 100 percent on the meeting. If you do these things, your success rate will go up. I guarantee it!

Once you have scheduled the meeting, make sure that you confirm the prospect's name, title, and address. Also make sure she has your name, your company name and telephone number! Repeat the date and time of the meeting at least twice. You want to make sure that you are both talking about the same date. In addition, as you give your prospect your name etc. and when you repeat the meeting date and time use your voice to direct your prospect to write everything down. Speak s-l-o-w-l-y and distinctly at a pace that they can write. Your prospect will interpret this way of speaking as a direction to write. This way they too will have the meeting in their calendar and there should be no mix-ups.

Appointment Setting Script for Printer/Graphic Arts Company

(*prospect's name*) please.

hi (*prospect's name*) my name is (*your name*) I'm with (*company name*)

we are a New York-based, full-service graphic arts company we specialize in print, production, design… we work with (*sounding bored*) (*customer name*), (*customer name*), and (*customer name*)… our work, of course, is terrific (*said lightly*) … but what's really important is (*pause*) we are educated, we are accommodating and we are (*emphasize*) reasonable people—and we know what we're doing!

we've been doing some work with (*client name*)—and when we first started working with them, all they were producing were some (*said with disdain*) not really terrific postcards… so we worked with them a little bit on image… we worked with them a little bit on positioning… (*matter of factly*) and they've more than doubled their revenue in the past year… (*nonchalantly and lightly*) I did say we know what we're doing…

(*said like it's a given and no big deal*) we'd like to introduce ourselves, meet with you for a few minutes, show you our portfolio, say "hi" and that way, in the future, if something comes up, you'll know us, you'll know our work… we need (*said like it's no big deal*) 10 minutes or so, whenever is good for you, do you have a few minutes later this week, or is next week better, whatever works for you…

Analysis

1. *Ask for the prospect by name*
   (***prospect's name***) please

2. *Say hello using the prospect's name*
   hi (***prospect's name***)

3. *Identify yourself and your company*
   my name is (***your name***). I'm with (***company name***)

4. *Say what you do (sound bite)*

   we are a New York-based, full-service graphic arts company

5. *Position yourself as the expert*

   we specialize in print, production, design… we work with (*customer name*), (*customer name*), and (*customer name*)… our work of course is terrific… but what's really important is we are educated, we are accommodating and we are reasonable people—and we know what we're doing!

6. *Success story to articulate customer benefits*

   we've been doing some work with (*client name*)—and when we first started working with them, all they were producing were some not really terrific postcards… so we worked with them a little bit on image… we worked with them a little bit on positioning… and they've more than doubled their revenue in the past year… I did say we know what we're doing…

7. *Ask for the meeting*

   we'd like to introduce ourselves, meet with you for a few minutes, show you our portfolio, say "hi" and that way, in the future, if something comes up, you'll know us, you'll know our work… we need 10 minutes or so, whenever is good for you, do you have a few minutes later this week, or is next week better, whatever works for you…

Summary: The Script Formula:

☎ Ask for the prospect by name

☎ Say hello. "Hi! Ms. Prospect" or "Hi Jane"

☎ Identify yourself and your company. "My name is
_____. My company is_____"

☎ Say what you do (sound bite)

☎ Position yourself as the expert. Use phrases like "we specialize in..." or "our reputation is..." "we are known for..." You can also do some name dropping of credentials here

☎ Describe your key selling points and clearly point out the Customer Benefits

☎ Tell a success story that is tailored to your prospect to help point out Customer Benefits

☎ Ask for what you want—an introductory meeting. "I would like to meet with you..." "I would like to introduce myself, my company, my product..." "I need 10 minutes of your time." "Is this Thursday good or would next Thursday be better?"

☎ Keep asking for what you want!

Chapter 7:
Getting It Right on the Phone

The rehearsal process is an essential part of being prepared. Many people have a lot of resistance to working with a script. The most frequent concern is that they will sound phony, like an actor, perhaps like they are reading. They worry that they cannot "be themselves" with a script. I would suggest that a script actually frees you to be yourself. You are prepared, you know your product, your selling points and customer benefits and you know what you want to achieve with the telephone call. You are ready for any objection your prospect may voice. You can relax—you can be yourself.

The written word and the spoken word are very different. Because you do not write the way you speak your script needs to be written to be read and performed in a real manner, in "people talk." It needs to be written in a conversational style, and delivered the way you actually speak. When you write your script leave out all capitalization and punctuation marks. Real people do not always speak in complete sentences and we do not talk the way we punctuate. So leave it out. If there is any section that you particularly wish to emphasize vocally, highlight or underline it. Work with a script in front of you. It will help to keep you focused. You do not have to memorize your script—although eventually with repetition you will—just keep it in front of you. And of course, do not read your script word for word; use your script as more of a guide and speak like a human being. If you are having a hard time writing your script—tape yourself, then write it down. Your script is fluid. It is not meant to be read word for word, but is an outline or a guide as to how you wish to represent yourself, your company or your product or service and what you want to accomplish.

In addition to a well-written, real-people-style script, the key to your performance is your delivery of that script. It is not just what you say—it's *how* you say it. To achieve the maximum effect with your delivery you will want to practice what you will say and practice different ways of saying it. Do this until you come up with the way that you think is most effective and will give you the result you want. This is your rehearsal process. If you are rehearsed, if you know what you want to say and how you want to say it, your words will flow. If you are not rehearsed you run the risk of stumbling and stammering—which will make you sound either like you are reading—or that you just don't know what you are talking about. You don't need to be an actor, but you do need to practice and rehearse your script until it flows easily. And rehearsal is a process. It takes time and repetition. What is wonderful about this process is that as you go through it, working on your script and rehearsing, your skills will improve.

Rehearsing means practicing your script *out loud* and not just "I'm going over it in my head." That's not good enough.

While practicing your script "in your head" is a type of visualization that can be useful, ultimately you have to practice *out loud* because you will be speaking with your prospect *out loud*. You must also work on the rhythm and timing of your delivery. (More on this later.) The idea here is to be so well rehearsed that you feel confident and prepared and free to be yourself. It is also a good idea to speak about your business or product/service as often as you can in "real life." You must get used to just talking about what you are doing. That skill will translate to the telephone.

I recently worked with a client who was very uncomfortable making introductory calls. Coincidentally, at the same time that I began working with her, she also started Internet Dating. She told me that the process of Internet Dating in many ways paralleled the introductory calling process. Every time she would meet a new date she would have to introduce herself, talk about her interests, her work... find out about the other person... This client said that even if she did not have a great date it was great practice for her telephone presentations! This client is now extremely successful at "getting in the door"—business-wise—and she's also successful in closing the sale once she gets there! (I don't know how well the dating is proceeding.)

Use a tape recorder during your rehearsal process. Tape yourself; listen to what you sound like. Do you sound like someone you would like to be having a conversation with? Listen closely to the tape and evaluate what you hear. Listen for warmth and passion in your voice. Do you sound interesting? Convincing? Confident? Is your speech clear, professional and pleasant? How is the rhythm and pacing of your speech? Or do you sound angry, tired, tentative or bored? Is your speaking voice nasal, a monotone or singsong? Do you speak too fast, or too slow? Do you mumble? Remember as you listen to the tape that you hear yourself differently than do others. By listening to your taped voice you will hear yourself as others hear you.

Next, ask a few friends or colleagues to listen to the tape. Ask them to evaluate it by the above criteria. Compare your friends' or colleagues' evaluations with yours. This way you will know how others perceive you. It may be different from your self-perceptions. Work on improving what you may need to improve. Try to work on just one element at a time. Otherwise it can be overwhelming.

Check List

Do you sound:	or	*Do you sound:*
Warm		Angry
Passionate		Bored/Tired
Interesting		Monotone
Confident/Convincing		Tentative
Professional		Unprofessional
Pleasant		Unpleasant
Clear		Unintelligible
Well Paced		Too fast or too slow
Well Pitched		Nasal, too high or singsong

In addition to taping yourself, it is also a good idea to practice with friends or colleagues. Call your friends and pitch them. Perhaps you can work with a colleague who is also making introductory calls. It is a good idea to do some role-playing. Practice your responses to prospect objections. Practice various sales scenarios. Then you will not have to worry about how you will deal with different objections or situations. You will have answers and be prepared. This leaves you free to really focus in on your prospect. Remember, the sales process is about your prospect, not about you. You want to be able to hear your prospect's concerns, needs and worries. You want to get a sense of the type of person with whom you are speaking. You cannot do any of this if you are worrying about yourself and what may come next.

Building rapport with your prospect starts with you and your prospect. Think about it—do you enjoy speaking with someone who is thinking about something else and not about your conversation? Of course you don't. People can sense when someone is not paying attention—your prospect will be able to tell whether you are focusing totally on your interaction with them or whether your mind is elsewhere. Do your preparation so that you can focus on your prospect and not worry about what your prospect may say later.

If you are worried that working with and rehearsing a script will make you sound "phony" remember that the best character that you can play is yourself. The script and rehearsal are so that you are prepared—not so that you can become an actor. Salespeople frequently are told to be "enthusiastic," but merely adding "enthusiasm" on top of the script will make you sound phony. Enthusiasm comes from within. It comes from integrity, believing in your product and/or service and being real. If you have these things and you work with your script and are prepared you will not sound phony!

Summary

☎ Write your script the way you speak

☎ Rehearse your script

 ◆ Practice out loud

 ◆ Work with a tape recorder

 ◆ Pitch your friends and colleagues

 ◆ Role play

☎ Be Yourself

☎ Building rapport begins with you and your prospect

☎ If you are new to or uncomfortable with introductory calling, start with your less-important leads

Chapter 8:
Terminating Telephone Terror

Fear

♦ They won't take my call

♦ They won't return my call

♦ They'll just say no

♦ I'll be disturbing them

♦ They are avoiding me

♦ They're too busy

♦ They probably already have a vendor or supplier

♦ I don't know what to say

This fear list could go on forever and is a combination of projection and distorted reality.

Reality

The truth is: prospects will take calls, you can get through, a lot of times they say "yes," you are not disturbing them (if you are, they will usually tell you and you can arrange to call back at a better time), and they are not too busy (again, if they are busy, they will usually tell you and you can arrange to call back at a better time). They are also not avoiding you—they don't know you. If they already have a vendor or supplier—that makes them a qualified prospect. They buy what you sell! And when you do your homework and write your script you will know what to say. It is true, however, that they will not return your calls. It is your job to call them.

What They Say Versus What You Hear

Part of active listening is to recognize that your priorities and your prospect's priorities are different. You want an immediate "yes," they may want to finish a report, a conversation, start their vacation.... Do not read negative or extra meaning into what is simply a different priority.

I have been working with a small business owner who I will call Cindy. She is just starting up her new business. I have been working with her on a marketing plan and coaching her on introductory calling, working to generate leads and new business. Cindy had scheduled a new business meeting with a prospect and when she called to confirm that meeting the prospect cancelled. This conversation with Cindy took place toward the end of March:

Cindy: I'm not going to follow up with XYZ Co. because when I called to confirm my meeting, her secretary said she had to meet with her accountant to finish her taxes and so she could not meet with me. I'm not going to follow up with this. She doesn't want to meet me. She must have her taxes done by now!

Wendy: I haven't done my taxes yet.

Cindy: Well, she doesn't want to meet with me because if she did, she would have kept the appointment.

Wendy: Maybe she really has to meet with her accountant and do her taxes.

This is a prime example of projection. The prospect says something, you hear something else. In this instance, Cindy's prospect said that she had to meet with her accountant. Cindy heard: "I don't want your product, I don't want to meet you, I don't want to do business with you." It is vitally important not to read extra meaning into statements made by prospects. Remember, your priorities and those of your prospect are not the same. Your number-one priority, of course, is getting in the door and ultimately making the sale. But that is not your prospect's number-one priority. She may not need your particular product or service until next week, next month or next year. Right now, she might have to do her taxes!

It is also important to separate yourself from whatever the prospect (or her secretary) says. This is not personal! It is business! It is sales! When you hear from the secretary that your prospect is "not available," "on the phone," "in a meeting," "out of the office"... this does not translate to: "My prospect knows that I am calling and she does not want to take my call. She doesn't like me. She doesn't want to buy from me. She doesn't want my product/service. She hates me." Generally what those phrases really mean are:

1. "She's not available" can mean:

    ♦ "She's sick today."

    ♦ "She's in the bathroom."

    ♦ "She left her desk for a moment."

    ♦ "She's not in today," etc.

2. "She's on the phone" means:

   She is talking on the telephone.

3. "She's out of the office" means:

   She is not in the office.

Assume that these phrases mean just what they say. Find out when your prospect will be available. Call back then. If your prospect says that she needs to cancel a meeting, do not assume that she is not interested. Assume instead she had a different priority at the moment and that she will reschedule. Remember: She did schedule the meeting in the first place. And let's do a little reality check here. Why would your prospect conspire to give you the runaround? If a prospect is genuinely not interested in a product and/or service she will tell you clearly. This does not mean rudely or meanly, just clearly. She will say, "I'm really not interested." Also remember: No matter what the secretary says (as long as secretaries are not your target market), the secretary is not the decision-maker.

Active listening also means listening to what interests your prospect. As discussed in Chapter 3, if during your conversation your prospect indicates an interest in a particular aspect of your product or service—that is what you need to focus on. That is their interest. Whether you believe that they are right or wrong is irrelevant. People buy for their reasons—not yours. Give them what they want.

When I am making introductory calls I always focus on the "yes's" and do not even hear "no's." If, for example, a prospect tells me that she is not the decision-maker, this is not a "no" and it is not a rejection! She is not the decision-maker, but most of the time she will tell me to whom I should be speaking—and that is a "yes!" She's helping me! If my prospect does not use my type of service, that is not a rejection! She does not use my type of service. All the common objections, "I'm too busy…" "Send me literature…" etc. are not necessarily rejections. Looking at introductory calling from this perspective gives me many "yes's" and very few "no's."

While there are many situations where it is important to simply take things at face value and move on, sometimes when a prospect voices an objection they do not voice their *total* objection. That is why you must listen actively. Through their objection the prospect is telling you something—but you must listen actively to ascertain what it is! Frequently the objection that your prospect voices hides their *real* objection. Your mission in this type of situation is to determine the real objection behind the spoken objection. You do this with answers that engage your prospect and help her voice her real thoughts. In this instance, rather than take things at face value you must listen for the underlying message. View an objection as information—not a rejection! More on this in Chapter 12, "Specific Answers to Specific Objections."

I recently worked with a client who had just begun making introductory calls. She told me that one day she made 30 calls and "got 29 rejections." So we analyzed those calls. On half of her calls that day she had only reached voice mail. Those calls were not rejections—they were voice mail. On another 5 calls my client spoke only with secretaries; the prospects were not in. These were not rejections—the prospects were not in. She did actually get valuable information from these 5 calls; she found out when to call back. Three prospects whom she did reach were not decision-makers and 3 did not use her type of service. Those weren't rejections: those prospects were not viable prospects. Three prospects indicated interest and asked her to call back. That is not rejection. At a later date, more than likely those three prospects will schedule introductory meetings. My client did schedule one new business meeting out of these calls and she also got some other valuable information. She learned that it takes 30 calls to schedule one new business meeting. As she continues to make calls, if the ratio stays at 30 calls to one appointment, then she will know that that is her sales cycle. It takes 30 calls to make one appointment. More than likely, however, as she continues to make calls her skills will improve and that ratio will lower. But it is a good idea to keep records of your calls so that you can determine your calls-to-appointments ratio.

The process of making introductory calls is very powerful and proactive. Why allow a stranger to determine your professional value or worth? Remember: these prospects are strangers! That is the definition of a cold call or an introductory call—calling strangers! They do not know you. If they do say "no" to you (and if you follow the above advice, they hardly ever will) you may choose, to never have to see them or speak with them again! (Although I do believe that if you have found what you consider to be a qualified prospect who says "no" to an introductory meeting you should nonetheless never let them go. Wait 6 months and try again—their situation may have changed.)

Whenever you avoid introductory calling you are probably thinking about it in a negative way. This creates unnecessary tension, stress and fear which impairs your ability to make introductory calls and increases the likelihood that you will fail. By thinking about introductory calling in this manner it is almost as if you are programming yourself to fail. Your expectations and mood profoundly influence what you do. Try this: Take 10 minutes each night before you fall asleep to visualize yourself making introductory calls, enjoying yourself and having success. Make up scripts for your prospects where they are happy to speak with you, very receptive and *want* to schedule an introductory meeting. This is your fantasy, so be creative. The important point here is to reprogram yourself to expect success, to expect a positive response from your prospects. The more you expect success, the more success you will have.

Few things are more terrifying than the unknown. The fear you create for yourself is far worse than the reality of introductory calling. Try breaking your fears down to the facts and the stories you tell yourself about those facts. For example: The facts are that you need to make introductory calls. You will call your prospect, speak with your prospect and ask for what you want—the appointment or the sale. The story is: You will be interrupting the prospect who will then be uninterested and rejecting. My introductory calling story goes like this: Prospects will be happy to hear from me. We will have an interesting and productive conversation. They will say "yes." Please use my introductory calling story until you develop one of your own.

Make a list of all of your fears, concerns, the stories you tell yourself. Calm down, think about it and then in a column right next to your fear list, write the rational response.

Reality Check List:

Fear:	Reality:
1. Prospects are rude.	Some prospects may be rude. Others may not.
2. They just say no.	But some do say yes!
3. They won't take my call.	Frequently they do.

Make your own Reality Check List. Carry a note pad with you and every time you think about introductory calling in a negative or fearful way make a note of the thought. Later, give your rational self a chance to counter with the reality. If you do this you can begin to talk back to yourself with positive, reality-based responses whenever you become fearful or anxious about your introductory calling.

Perhaps I've been toughened by years of auditioning—at a dance audition sometimes the people in charge of the audition won't even let you dance! Sometimes they simply line everyone up, look at you and then say "Thank you—you can leave." This is called "typing," and if you're too short, too tall, have the wrong hair color or won't fit the costume, it doesn't matter how well you dance.

As a teenager I went to a scholarship audition for the Harkness Ballet School. I did not get the scholarship; they said I was a very talented dancer—but my back was too long. Some things are under your control and some things are not. I could not do anything about the length of my back. But what I could do, what was under my control was to continue to dance, to study at other schools and to continue to audition.

If a prospect does say "no" ultimately that is out of your control—but what is within your control is continuing to prospect and continuing to make introductory calls. Too many people focus on the rejection. Yes, occasionally there is rejection, but if you think about it in a different manner you can focus on the "yes's" and leave the "no's" behind.

The truth is that most people you speak with will be very nice, and if they use your product or service they will appreciate your call. If they do not use your product or service, they will tell you that. If they are not the decision-maker, generally they will tell you who to speak with. Once you have qualified your lead, she may have objections to meeting or buying your product or service, but that is a different story and will be dealt with later. Occasionally you may speak with someone who is rude. This has nothing to do with you. Do not take it personally. They do not know you; perhaps they are just having a bad day. Whatever the reason, it is neither your fault nor your problem. Move on.

Arlene's Game

If, however, you feel that you are unable to let go of feeling rejected—try this. Go for the rejections—be 100 percent committed to being rejected. I am indebted to my friend Arlene Love for this idea. She does not make introductory calls; she is an actress and she uses this method for her auditions and just for life in general. So I call this *Arlene's Game*. The goal in *Arlene's Game* is to reach 100 points. You get 1 point for every rejection. In Arlene's case, when she goes to an audition, if she does not get the part she gives herself 1 point. For every audition she goes to and every part she does not get, she gives herself 1 point. If she does get the part—well that's a big bonus! If she does not get the part, however, she is playing the game and compiling points.

You can play *Arlene's Game* too. Take a piece of paper and write down the numbers 1 to 100. Give yourself 1 point for every "no" answer you get when asking a prospect for a meeting. If your prospect agrees to the meeting—well consider that to be a bonus! In the meantime focus entirely on acquiring points. Every time you get a "no" cross out a number. The more calls you make, the more points you can acquire. When you reach 100 points—You Win! Give yourself a nice prize! Take yourself out to dinner or perhaps just sleep an extra hour in the morning. Make the prize something that you really consider to be a prize. And make sure that you actually accept and take your prize!

One of my recent clients told me she really turned the corner and began to be successful with her introductory calling when she realized that when she reached 100 points playing *Arlene's Game* she could go shopping! And she loves to shop! So make sure to give yourself a prize that's really a prize.

If you have reached 100 points playing *Arlene's Game* also give yourself a big pat on the back because in order to get 100 points and win you have to have made many, many introductory calls. Part of the process of making introductory calls is just numbers; the more introductory calls that you make, the more success you will have. In addition, if you have only one prospect to pursue, that prospect becomes overwhelmingly important. If you have hundreds of leads, no one prospect can make or break you. So if you are playing *Arlene's Game* and compiling points you are making a lot of introductory calls. You are sure to have "yes's" sprinkled in with the "no's." Once you reach 100 points, immediately start compiling your next 100 points.

Top Ten Tips for Terminating Telephone Terror

1. *Make telephone calls*

   Few things are more terrifying than the unknown. The fear you create for yourself is far worse than the reality of introductory calling. Once you start making telephone calls and continue making telephone calls it gets easier. You overcome fear by doing.

2. *Make a lot of telephone calls*

   If you have only one prospect to pursue, that prospect becomes overwhelmingly important. If you have hundreds of leads, no one prospect can make or break you. The more calls you make, the more success you will have.

3. *Prepare*

   Prepare for introductory calling the way you would for any major presentation. Know what you want to say, how you want to say it and how you want to represent yourself, your company, your product or service. And know the goal of your telephone call.

4. *Practice*

   If you are new to introductory calling or uncomfortable with introductory calling practice your pitch *out loud*. Role-play with friends or colleagues. Practice various sales scenarios. This way you will not have to worry about what you are going to say, you will be prepared and you can focus in on your prospect.

5. *Start with less important leads*

   It will be good practice and less stressful. Once you feel more comfortable, start working on the more important leads.

6. *Stay calm*

   You will for the most part be talking to people who will appreciate your call. If a prospect is rude, remember: This is not personal. They may just be having a bad day. Move on.

7. *Your priorities and your prospect's priorities are different*

   You want an immediate "yes," your prospect may want to finish a report, finish a conversation, start their vacation.... Be very careful not to read negative or extra meaning into early conversations with your prospect or prospect's secretary. If, for example, your prospect's secretary says that your prospect is "on the phone," "in a meeting" or "out of the office," that does not translate to "My prospect knows that I am calling and is avoiding me."

8. *Some things are out of your control*

   If a prospect does say "no" ultimately that is out of your control—but what is within your control is continuing to prospect and continuing to make calls. It is also within your control to improve your cold calling skills, take seminars, read books or hire a coach—then fewer prospects will say "no."

9. *Arlene's Game*

   The object of *Arlene's Game* is to focus on rejection. The goal is to reach 100 points. You get 1 point for every rejection. Give yourself 1 point for every "no" answer. If your prospect says "yes," that's a bonus! Focus on acquiring points. The more calls you make, the more points you acquire. When you reach 100—You Win! Give yourself a prize!

10. *Have fun*

   This is not life or death—it's only an introductory call. The fate of the world does not rest on you and your telephone. You will not destroy your company or ruin your life if a prospect says "no." Loosen up, be creative, have some fun!

Summary

☎ Reality check:

- ◆ Prospects will take calls
- ◆ A lot of times they say "yes"
- ◆ They are not too busy
- ◆ They are not avoiding you
- ◆ If they have a vendor or supplier they are a qualified prospect!
- ◆ When you write your script—you will know what to say
- ◆ Your prospect will not return your calls—it is your job to call them

☎ Your priorities and your prospect's priorities are different

☎ This is not personal!

☎ Listen actively to ascertain what your prospect is really saying

☎ Listen for the "yes's"

☎ If listening for the "yes's" does not work for you—try *Arlene's Game*

Chapter 9:
Naming Your Prospect

Your business is with the decision-maker and only the decision-maker. The receptionist, secretary or assistant (unless they are your target market) cannot make the decision to purchase your product or service. There is therefore no need to explain yourself to them. The best way to put a name on the decision-maker and also to get through the screens is to stay anonymous and undercover. You are not being rude—remember that part of the receptionist, secretary or assistant's job is to help you and to put your call through. Remember also that you are calling because your customer or prospect needs you, and you have something of value to offer.

If you have completed your Customer Profile you will have noticed similarities in types of businesses that use your product/service and similarities in the titles of the decision-makers who may purchase your product or service. If the title of the decision-maker for your particular product/service is generally "Senior Vice President of Whatever," it is a pretty good bet that if you call a similar type of business the title of the decision-maker will be something like "Senior Vice President of Whatever."

Once you have identified that area or title, you want to find the *highest level* person that you think may be the decision-maker. If that person is not actually the decision-maker, they can probably tell you who is the decision-maker.

If you are calling a larger company the screening process is generally in two parts, first the receptionist screen and then the secretary or assistant screen. (I will talk about voice mail in Chapter 13.) To name the decision-maker you will start with the receptionist screen. If you are calling a smaller company, the person who answers the telephone, the receptionist, may double as the secretary—or may even be the owner of the company! In this type of situation you will use a combination of receptionist and secretary/assistant screening techniques. But for now, let us begin with the receptionist.

When you are making introductory calls you should expect to speak with your prospect. You have something of value that is of benefit to your prospect, something your prospect needs—of course she would wish to speak with you! If you cannot immediately adopt this attitude, try thinking about it like this:

If Gwyneth Paltrow were to call Steven Spielberg at Dreamworks and ask to speak with Steven Spielberg the Dreamworks operator might say: "What is this in reference to?" Gwyneth would never reply:

> "I'm an actress…. You know—*Shakespeare in Love, Sliding Doors*…."

She would instead say:

"This is Gwyneth Paltrow—is he available?"

Her expectation would be that her call would be put through to Steven Spielberg and that Steven Spielberg would want to speak with her.

On an introductory call your attitude should be just like Gwyneth's. Expect your call to be put through and that your prospect will want to speak with you. If you do not like the Gwyneth persona make up your own! But remember—this conversation is to your prospect's benefit!

Five Ways to Name the Prospect

1. *Ask the receptionist*

   The easiest way to name your prospect is to simply ask the receptionist. A part of her job is to help you identify the prospect. The other part of her job is to connect you. (Generally, receptionists are underpaid and overworked. Callers are frequently rude, so be very nice to the receptionist; she can be a tremendous help! If you are trying to get information and the receptionist is busy, say, "I know you're very busy, I'll hold." And make sure to thank her for her help!)

You: "Before you connect me, (P A U S E) I need to reach…" (give title) "Who is that please?"

(The key words here are: "before" and "reach." You say, "Before you connect me" and then you pause because you want the receptionist to hear the word "before" and that way give you a name before she puts you through. The word "reach" is vague, which I like. You could be writing a letter or you could wish to speak directly with the prospect.)

Receptionist: "What is this in reference to?"

(This "What is this in reference to?" is different than later on when the secretary or assistant says it. At this point the receptionist doesn't really mean what is this in reference to? She means I do not understand what you want, there is no one here by that title, I don't know who to connect you with. Remember: Her job is to connect you with someone.)

You: *(Use the "Broken Record Technique"—Repeat what you just said but elaborate a little. For example, if you want to reach the Senior Vice President of Marketing:)* I need to reach whoever handles marketing. I don't know if that would be your Senior Vice President of Marketing or your Marketing Director or your Advertising Director…. Who would handle that and what is the correct title?

(If you keep using the "Broken Record Technique" and throwing out titles, eventually the receptionist will latch onto one and give you a name. Ask for the correct spelling. Ask: "Does she have a direct line?" Ask, "What is the exact title?")

Sometimes if a company has a policy that they will not give out names at the switchboard you can ask to be connected with that department. When the receptionist in that area answers you start over with "Before you connect me..." At this point, you may have to use a combination of receptionist and secretary screening techniques. I explain how in the following chapter.

2. *Call the Chief Executive Officer*

   The theory here is that Executive Secretaries know everything. Call the CEO's office. Ask for the CEO. When the Executive Secretary says, "What is this in reference to?" tell her. She will then generally point you in the right direction, in addition to which when you get to your prospect you can say, "the CEO's office said I should be meeting with you," implying that you actually spoke with the CEO. Make sure you get a telephone number, etc.

3. *Randomly change the numbers of the general switchboard number*

   If the general number is -5000, call -5001, -5002, -5003 etc. and keep going until you actually reach a human being. Ask them to help you. "Would you help me please?" People love to help. Ask: "Who is in charge of that department?" "Who is the liaison with...?" "Who should I speak with?" "Who would handle that?" Once you get a name, ask: "Do you have a company directory? Would you look up that extension for me?" Sometimes they will, sometimes they won't—but it never hurts to ask.

4. *The made-up name*

   If asking the receptionist the first time doesn't work because company policy forbids them to give out names, make up a name and ask the receptionist for that person. The receptionist will say, "There is no one by that name here." You will say, "Oh, Jane Jones used to be the Senior Vice President of Whatever. She was the one I always dealt with. Who has taken over for her?" Assuming that the receptionist has not been at the company since the beginning of time and knows there was never any Jane Jones... she may very well give you the prospect's name.

5. *A last resort*

   Call Human Resources. Use the same technique that you use with the receptionist. "Before you connect me...."

Summary

☎ Call the highest-level person who you think is the decision-maker

☎ Your expectation is that your prospect will take your call

☎ Five ways to name the prospect:

1. Ask the receptionist
2. Call the Chief Executive Officer
3. Randomly change the numbers of the general switchboard number
4. Ask for a made-up name
5. As a last resort call Human Resources

Chapter 10:
Getting Past the Palace Guard

Sometimes reaching your prospect by telephone can be like getting an audience with the Queen. A moat surrounds the castle, the drawbridge is up and there is a uniformed armed guard at every entrance. What do you do?

As with the receptionist, here you also want to stay undercover. Your business is with the decision-maker and only the decision-maker. Neither the secretary nor the assistant can make the decision to purchase your product or service, so there is no real reason to engage with them. Their job is to put you through to their boss.

Your mission is to either:

♦ Get the decision-maker on the telephone or

♦ Find out when you can reach the decision-maker and call back then

This is how you do it:

You: *Ask for your prospect by name. You can do this because you have already named the decision-maker.* "Jane Jones, please."

Screen: "Who's calling?"

You: *Give your name or, better yet, give your name and say,* "Is she available?" *You want to know whether or not the prospect is available. If the prospect is not available you want to find out when she may be available and call back then. If you ask,* "Is she available?" *the screen may at this point simply tell you,* "Oh, she's in a meeting." *At which point you ask,* "When will she be done with the meeting?" *then get off of the phone and call back when the screen said the meeting would be finished.*

Sometimes, however, the screening process just continues...

Screen: "What company are you calling from?"

You: *Give your company name. You can also ask again,* " Is she available?" *If your company name says what you do (example, ABC Printing Co.), it is a good idea to make your company name unidentifiable and simply say* "ABC." *You can also add the word* "Group" *to your company name, making your company sound like a group of investors (The ABC Group). The idea here is to stay undercover until you get the decision-maker on the telephone.*

At this point the screen may ask additional questions:

Screen: "What is (company name)?"

"What is this in reference to?"

"I need more information."

"I need to screen her calls".

"What is this concerning?"

"Does she know you?"

Your answer to any question is along these lines:

You: "Please tell Jane Jones (*the secretary's boss*) that (*your name*) from (*your company*) is on the line." *This is an incredibly simple response, yet it takes the decision-making power of whether or not to put your call through out of the hands of the secretary. This gives her something to do—you've basically made a request—and then allows her boss to make the decision whether or not to pick up the telephone. More often than not, if the boss is available she will pick up the phone.*

To avoid all these questions simply cut to the chase. When she says, "Who's calling?" you say, "Please tell Jane Jones (*the secretary's boss*) that (*your name*) from (*your company*) is on the line."

Your screen may still say:

Screen: "I need more information."

You: "This is really quite complex and it is something that I need to discuss with Jane Jones. Is she available?" *Again, you want to either get the prospect on the telephone or find out when the prospect will be available and call back then.*

If the screen continues to give you a hard time, you can simply say "Please tell Jane Jones (*the secretary's boss*) that (*your name*) is on the line. I believe that will be fine." *Usually it is. Again you are asking the screen to do something and taking the decision-making power out of her hands. While you are not actually saying that you know her boss, you are definitely implying that you do. And once the screen relays your information to her boss, more often than not, if she is available, she will pick up the telephone. If she is not available, at this point the secretary will probably tell you (she's in a meeting, out of the office, etc.), and you can go on to the next call. Attitude is the key here. Remember you are Gwyneth Paltrow! You can also sound slightly annoyed. Gwyneth would certainly be annoyed that her name was not recognized. The tone also instructs the screen that your call should go through.*

Once you have the prospect on the line, start your pitch...

If your prospect is unavailable:
- ◆ She's on the phone.
- ◆ She's away from her desk.
- ◆ She's in a meeting.
- ◆ She's out of the office.
- ◆ She's not available.

Remember, you will take all of these statements at face value.

Screen: "She's on the phone," *or* "She's away from her desk." *Most people are on the phone or away from their desk for only a few minutes.*

You: "I'll call back in a few minutes." *Wait 5 to 10 minutes and then call back.*

Screen: "She's out of the office."

"She's not available."

"She's in a meeting."

You: "When will she be finished with that meeting?"

"When will she return?"

"What time do you expect her?"

"When is the best time to reach her?" *You can give choices of time here. This allows the secretary to pick one, making it easier for her.*

"What time in the morning does she come in?" *You can give choices of time here. Again, this allows the secretary to pick one, making it easier for her.*

"How late will she be in this afternoon?"

Screen: "She's at lunch."

You: "When will she return?" *If the screen does not know, try calling back in one hour.*

When speaking with a screen, remember to always use directed words such as: What or When…. If you ask "Do you know what time…?" the screen can simply answer "Yes" or

"No." However, with directed words, if she knows, she must give you an answer.

Some Other Responses That Are Useful

Screen: "Does she know what this is in reference to?"

You: *Try and sound slightly amused here.* "She may not. Please tell Jane Jones... etc...."

Screen: "What is this in reference to?"

You: *If you have forwarded materials, either before the introductory call (but please don't do this anymore!) or at your prospect's request after the initial call—*"We've had correspondence. Please tell Jane Jones... etc...."

Screen: "Would you like to leave a message?"

You: "I'm going into a meeting. I'll call her back."

"I'll be out of the office. I'll call her back."

You are letting the screen know that her boss will not be able to return the telephone call. This makes sense, and most secretaries or assistants will accept it. Messages are an absolute last resort. It is unlikely anyone will ever call you back. Don't expect it. It is your job to reach the prospect! These days a lot of people have voice mail, and getting to the decision-maker can be frustrating. Chapter 13 explains how to work around voice mail. You can also say "I won't bother you with a message, I'll just call back." Many secretaries are appreciative of this and say "Thank you!"

If the screen is very insistent about taking a message, and sometimes they are:

Screen: "I have to know what this is in reference to when you call back."

You: "I'll be happy to give you whatever you need when I call back." *Of course when you do call back you'll start again with* "Please tell Jane Jones..."

The Receptionist/Secretary

If you are calling a smaller company, chances are the receptionist will also act as the secretary/screen. If this is your first call to this company and you are trying to name the decision-maker, you will use a combination of receptionist/secretary screening techniques. Start with "Before you connect me..." Once you have a name, switch to "Please tell Jane Jones..." The key here is to stay focused. Your agenda is to name and then reach the decision-maker. The receptionist/secretary will have a different agenda. Stay focused and committed at all times to your agenda and this works.

Occasionally, when you call a smaller company your prospect will answer the telephone. If you use the *Broken Record Technique* and name various areas or departments (i.e. Promotions, Purchasing...) where the decision to purchase your product or service is usually made in other companies, the prospect will often say, "I handle that." Introduce yourself, start your pitch.

Summary

☎ Your mission:

1. Get the decision-maker on the telephone or
2. Find out when you can reach the decision-maker and call back then

☎ Ask for your prospect by name

☎ Give your name and company name

☎ If the prospect is available say: "Please tell Jane Jones (*the secretary's boss*) that (*your name*) from (*your company*) is on the line"

☎ If your prospect is not available, ask directed questions: ("When will she return?" "What time is she done with that meeting?") to establish when to call back

☎ Do not leave messages

☎ With smaller companies, use a combination of receptionist and secretary/assistant screening techniques

Chapter 11:
Qualifying the Decision-Maker

How do you decide if a prospect really is the right prospect? And how do you make sure that the person you are pitching is actually in a position to make a decision about purchasing your product or service?

Generally if you ask, "Are you the person who purchases..." the response will be, "What are you selling?" "Send some literature" or simply "I'm not interested." And that will be that.

When you created your marketing plan you established whom you need to call, the type of business and the usual title of the decision-maker. If you have done your homework, you should, more or less, be in the right area to find the decision-maker. Call the highest-level person that you can in your targeted area. If that person is not the correct person, generally they will know who is because generally that person will be reporting to them. You should have also developed your qualifying questions to ask your prospect, questions whose answers will confirm that you are indeed speaking with the decision-maker. Examples could be: "How often do you use this type of service?" "Who is your current vendor?" "What are your concerns about this service?" Everyone will have different qualifying questions. You need to decide what makes a prospect qualified to do business with you.

Allow Your Prospect to Self-Qualify

An introductory call will be more effective if you allow your prospects to qualify themselves. I believe that you need to earn the right to start asking questions. If you call your prospect and right away start interrogating, they will probably not be inclined to answer. Would you be? A better way is to use your script. Introduce yourself, your company, and your product... give your pitch, then ask for what you want—a meeting. (Remember, at this moment you are not selling your product or service, you are selling an appointment, a meeting. You want a few minutes of their time. This is not a big deal.) If this prospect is a qualified prospect she will generally let you know either by scheduling the meeting or starting to offer objections. If your prospect immediately says "yes" to a meeting, set the date and then qualify further by asking your *already prepared* qualifying questions. If, on the other hand, your prospect offers objections first, in the course of answering those objections you can also qualify further by working your questions into the ensuing conversation. Or you can answer the objection, set the meeting date and then, as above, ask your qualifying questions. Phrase the qualifying questions in terms of "to better prepare for our meeting..."

If this prospect is not the decision-maker the conversation may go something like this: They will ask (probably sounding a little confused) "Why are you calling me?" Explain you are calling to introduce yourself and your product or service, repeat your sound bite that says what you do, then ask if they use your product or service. If they say "no" ask: "Whom should I speak with? Who would handle this?" More than likely you'll get a name. (Ask for their phone number, too!) Make sure you use directed words. Ask "Whom should I speak with?" and not "Do you know whom I should speak with?" With the first question, if they know, they must give you a name. With the second question, they could simply answer "yes." If your now invalid prospect simply names another department or area without mentioning a potential prospect name, ask: "Who is in charge of that area?" or "Who is in charge of that department?" Remember—you want the highest-level person you can find—that way if they are not your true prospect, they can tell you who is. Once you have a name, start over with this new prospect. Sometimes finding the decision-maker is like going through a maze, but it can be done. It requires patience and persistence.

When you have reached the decision-maker you will know. They will ask appropriate questions and have answers to your qualifying questions which you ask after they have agreed to the meeting. If you are still not sure, you can ask: "Who else is involved in this decision?" Other questions might be:

"What is the decision-making process?"

"What is your role in the decision-making process?"

"How have decisions been made in the past?"

When you ask your qualifying questions, avoid questions that imply that your prospect has made mistakes in their past decisions. For example:

"What don't you like about your current vendor?"

"What are the weaknesses of your current supplier?"

Both of these questions imply an insult to your prospect's decision-making abilities. Better questions might be:

"What would you like that you're not getting now?"

"What areas could improve?"

If your prospect already has a vendor, a particularly useless question is:

"How is that working for you?" (or "How is that going?")

A better approach is to ask about specific problems—that you know you can solve:

"When (*fill in the blank*) happens, how do you handle it?"

"What are you doing about (*fill in the blank*)?"

Try not to ask your prospect what they like about their current vendor. This approach can backfire and sell them once again on their current supplier!

Summary

☎ Find the highest-level person in the right area

☎ Allow your prospect to self-qualify. Let your prospect tell you that she is the decision-maker

☎ Give your pitch

☎ Ask your qualifying questions

☎ If necessary, qualify further with questions about the prospect's decision-making role

☎ Be patient and persistent

Chapter 12:
Specific Answers to
Specific Objections

1. I already have a vendor/supplier

If your prospect already has a vendor, that automatically qualifies them as a prospect! They use your product or service. The more vendors they have for a particular product or service, the more business they are doing—therefore the better the prospect! Here are three possible responses:

You: "...you never know what may happen in the future, and I'd like to introduce myself and (*company name and/or product*)..., that way, if your situation changes or something comes up you'll know me (*product/ service*)..."

or

You: "...you never know what might happen in the future, it certainly never hurts to have a backup source..."

or

You: "...you never know what might happen in the future, perhaps you may need a supplement to your current vendor or supplier."

or

Any combination of the above answers.

Then ask for the meeting again.

2. Send literature

This is an objection that prospects say when they really mean something else. This objection hardly ever means that your prospect is going to sit down and read your materials. Generally this objection means (a) you haven't convinced me or (b) I'm too busy. The idea here is to get your prospect to reveal their true objection which you can then address. Here are two possible responses:

You: "I have some information that I could put in the mail to you. It's going to take you 10 minutes to read it and I really only need 10 minutes of your time." *Then ask for the meeting again.*

or

You: "I'm a walking, talking brochure." *Then ask for the meeting again.*

or

You can also use a combination of the two.

You: "I'm a walking, talking brochure… and it's going to take you 10 minutes to read any literature that I might send, and I really only need 10 minutes of your time." *Then ask for the meeting.*

When you give this response your prospect will usually come out with their true objection, which you can then address.

122

Send literature only as support—never as introduction.

Some people like to send marketing materials as an introduction before their call. They feel that this will somehow "warm up the call." I believe that prospects rarely read your literature. More often than not it is thrown away or sits in a pile on their desk. Then when you call them either they haven't read it, they don't remember it or they've lost it—so you have to send your materials again! Make the human connection first, and then send marketing materials or samples as necessary. If after making the telephone contact your prospect wants these materials, by all means send them and send them *right away*! If your prospect has said "no"— they do not really need any materials. This approach will save time and cut expenses, you will not be printing as many brochures, sending as many samples or paying for as much postage!

Sending materials before the initial call can actually decrease your chances of getting in the door. It makes it possible for your prospect to say "I've got your materials on file. I'll call you if I need you." If you call first, and your prospect absolutely, positively insists on receiving written material, this gives you a second chance to call her back and try for that meeting. Sometimes you can promise to send literature immediately and at the same time suggest that you both "pencil in a meeting" for a few weeks later, after they have had a chance to review the materials. This way everyone gets what they want!

I like the word "pencil" because it implies that it is not a solid meeting—it can be erased or rescheduled. This way your prospect won't feel trapped. You get what you want (a meeting), they get what they want (written information and low pressure—if something comes up they can reschedule).

3. I'm too busy

This is also an objection that means something else. This is not a "no." Instead, think of this as a "yes"—you just have to find the right time.

This objection is also an example of "what you say versus what they hear." Because what your prospect frequently hears, especially if they are very busy, when you say that you would like to introduce yourself is: "I'm downstairs and I'm coming up *now*." You need to reassure your prospect that you will meet with her at her convenience. This will assuage the pressure your prospect may feel.

You: "I only need 10 minutes of your time, whenever is good for you." *Find out when the prospect might be available and schedule for then, or call back at that time.*

4. I'm too busy this week (or the next several weeks)

This is definitely *not* a rejection—you are only negotiating *when*!

You: "When do you expect your time to free up? You tell me what looks good for you."

When your prospect mentions some future possible time you then say:

You: "Why don't we pencil something in for… (*some time in advance*). It's not chiseled in stone, and if it doesn't work out, we can always reschedule."

5. Call me back in 2 weeks (3 weeks, whatever)

You: "I'd be happy to, or let's pencil something in for 2 weeks from now. It's not chiseled in stone. I'll be happy to give you a call to confirm, and if it doesn't work out, we can always reschedule."

Here is a technique that I have only recently discovered. I am finding, however, that it works very well! If your prospect asks you to call back at a later date:

You: "Let's pencil something in for 2 weeks from now (*or whatever the date mentioned by your prospect*)... And of course, it's not chiseled in stone. I will give you a call to confirm, and if it's not going to work, we'll figure out something else... but this way, I'll have the time carved out on *my* calendar.

This works because while agreeing to schedule the meeting, your prospect does not feel trapped. At the same time, you are accommodating her by working with her calendar; she then feels compelled to accommodate you—especially since you are being very low key about the whole thing.

Once someone has scheduled a meeting they are more likely to keep it, or if that scheduled time turns out not to work, they are more likely to reschedule. Also—why make an extra phone call if you don't have to?

The Guilt Technique: Use this on your second call when your prospect has insisted that you call back at a later date.

You: "Hi, Ms. Prospect! We spoke on (*give date*) and you were (*fill in the blank...very busy, in a meeting etc.*) But you said I should call back and that you would be able to carve out a few minutes for me to introduce myself (*company, product...*)." *Then again, ask for the meeting.*

6. Your Product/Service Is Too Expensive

Price objections are relative issues. Before you jump in and explain to your prospect why your price is reasonable you need to know what the price comparison is that your prospect is making. "Too expensive" compared to what? Generally there are two basic price objections—either you are perceived as being more expensive than your competition or you are perceived as too expensive in relation to your prospect's budget. Either way, you need information.

One excellent information-gathering technique is to repeat your prospect's objection back to them. If your prospect says your product/service is "too expensive," repeat the objection—being careful not to sound argumentative or hostile, just genuinely interested. "Too expensive?" Then be quiet. Let your prospect explain exactly what "too expensive" means. Another good technique is to simply ask, "Why do you say that?" Again, let your prospect explain.

The best way to overcome a price objection is to anticipate it and preempt it before it ever happens. If you are consistently hearing from prospects that your product/service is "too expensive" then it is imperative to change how you talk about your product or service. Establish your expertise by clearly defining what it is that makes you and/or your company different from the competition. Set yourself apart— then address the issue of "too expensive."

If your product or service is genuinely more expensive than your competition there should be valid reasons for that difference—define those reasons. Your job is to establish value, not price. If your widget costs $100 and lasts for 6 years, and your competitor's widget only costs $50 but lasts for just 1 year, which is the better value? If, on the other hand, the price objections you hear seem to be budgeting issues, make sure to include information on pricing or payment options up front.

7. I Am, or Have Been, Dissatisfied with Your Product/Service

Ask what happened. Apologize briefly: "I'm sorry to hear that." Or "I'm sorry that you had that experience." Let them talk and try to analyze the facts. Ask what you can do to make it up. Offer something extra. Ask for their input. People do enjoy being asked for help or advice. Ask for another chance. And above all, be sincere, honest and courteous!

8. I never make appointments

This one is my personal favorite because it's kind of silly. Clearly in situations where they feel a need, prospects do make appointments. When a prospect says this what they are really saying is "you haven't convinced me, you haven't sold me." Your mission, if a prospect says this, is to try to uncover their real objection and address it. Try giving their statement back to them.

You: "Never?" *(Spoken in a soft, yet slightly incredulous tone)*

Sometimes prospects will make statements like "I never make appointments." Or "We never use that service." Or "We won't change our supplier." If you believe your prospect to be a qualified prospect, you cannot take these types of objections at face value. They are probably masking other real objections, but you need more information in order to know what those objections are. Your goal is to get your prospect talking. Give the statement back to them and then shut up! "Never?" or you can say "Really?" Often this starts your prospect talking, and they will express their real objection that you can then address. You must be careful not to sound hostile or argumentative when you use this technique. Instead, sound gentle and a little surprised but very, very interested.

9.   I can't take the time to meet with every vendor/salesperson who calls

If you are hearing this a lot, the problem is in your script. If in your script you are able to position yourself as the expert you will preempt this objection because you will have set yourself and your company apart from just any vendor/salesperson. If a prospect says this to you before you have fixed your script, go back to the idea of "you never know what might happen in the future..." and then try and draw your prospect out with some questions that will give you a chance to discover your prospect's concerns and another chance to try to schedule that meeting.

Recently I had occasion to cold call and meet with a distributor for this book. We had a very good meeting. At the end of the meeting we were chatting and he began to tell me how annoying cold callers and telemarketers are. He said he never meets with someone who cold calls. There I sat with a book called *Cold Calling for Women*, having cold called him myself, but in his mind he had taken me out of the category of "annoying cold caller" and placed me in the category of "someone with something of value to offer." I was no longer "every salesperson who calls." If your script works well, you too will no longer be "every salesperson who calls."

10. I'm not interested

Again, if you are hearing this a lot, the problem is either in your script or in your delivery. If prospects are continually telling you they are not interested—then you are not saying anything that is interesting! Do some brainstorming here. Ask colleagues for advice. Tape yourself, listen to how you sound. Are you speaking clearly? Is there energy in your voice? It is also a good idea to go to some of your customers, ask for their help. Tell them what you are trying to do and ask what would catch their interest? Try different approaches until you come up with a solution.

If you are on the telephone with a prospect who says "I'm not interested" try very softly and gently, "Really?" This may get your prospect to open up and give you more information about what does interest her. This kind of information can help you make your approach more appealing.

Another thing you might try if your prospect says she's "not interested":

You: I understand that you are not interested at the moment, but maybe you can help me. I believe that I have a very, very good product (*service, company...*) here, yet you are not the first person to tell me that they are not interested. Maybe I'm not explaining myself very well. What could I tell you about this product (*service, company...*) that you *would* find interesting?

Let your prospect tell you. They may very well give you the information that you need to sell them, or at the very least, information that you can use in the future.

If one prospect says, "I'm not interested," it may be just an aberration, but if you are hearing this a lot, stop calling and work on your script.

11. I'll call you

Sometimes a prospect will agree that a meeting is a good idea, but they say they are too busy and will call you. They will never call you—it is your job to call them. Simply say: "I know you're very busy, I'll just plan on touching base in a few days (*few weeks, months… whatever the time frame the prospect has mentioned*) in case I haven't heard from you." If your prospect does call it's a bonus! If not—call your prospect again.

(NOTE: If your prospect is being rude you can ask, very gently and softly, "Ms. Prospect, have I offended you in some way?" They will then usually tell you what is going on and why they are reacting in that manner.)

Success Story

Once, while representing one of my clients, I had a conversation with a prospect that went something like this… I gave my pitch, asked for the meeting and the prospect replied:

Prospect: "I already have 15 vendors." *I thought to myself "Bingo!—Qualified Prospect!"*

Wendy: "We always figure that you never know what might happen in the future and we would just like to introduce ourselves."

Prospect: "Send literature."

Wendy: "I do have some information that I could send to you, but it will take you 10 minutes to look through it and we only need 10 minutes of your time. We're a walking, talking brochure!"

Prospect: "I've already received samples from representatives from your company." *At this point he opened his Rolodex and started reading out names of sales representatives, many of whom were no longer with the company.*

Wendy: "That is exactly my point. A sample is just a sample—it's the people who put the work together who make the difference. We'd like you to meet someone who still actually works here."

Prospect: "I'm too busy."

Wendy: "We only need 10 minutes of your time, whenever is good for you. Is next week good? Would the week after be better—because we only need 10 minutes of your time."

Prospect: "I never make appointments."

Wendy: "Never? Never, ever?"

The prospect scheduled the meeting and my client did get a new customer! Now, why did this work? This prospect never said to me: "No, I'm not interested." What he actually did was signal his interest by continuing the conversation. What that meant to me was that I had simply not offered the right argument yet—I had not yet convinced him to schedule the meeting. But as long as he stayed on the line, I was going to give it my best shot. He wasn't saying "no," he was saying "convince me!"

I believe that the prospect who gives you the most trouble is frequently the prospect you want! Once you turn this prospect into a client or customer, they will be just as loyal to you and will give other callers the same objections that you heard. Others will not be as tenacious or skilled as you; therefore you will have this customer for a very long time.

Being persistent and tenacious shows dedication and commitment. This demonstrates to your prospect/customer how you will tackle a project for them, that you will "go to the wall" to get it done, just as you did when making the introductory call and scheduling the introductory meeting. Your prospects will respect you for your conviction and persistence!

Summary

☎ Ask for a meeting. Keep asking for a meeting

☎ Initial prospect objections frequently mask the real objections. Part of your response must be to help your prospect tell you their real objection that you can then address

☎ Prospect objections are a way of getting information about your prospect. Use the objections to get your prospect talking

☎ Be persistent

Chapter 13:
Why Don't They Return My Calls; Voice Mail; and Other Miscellaneous Information

Why Don't They Return My Calls?

Forget it, they just don't. No prospect will ever call you back. And why should they? It is your job to call your prospect. This rule applies when you are working from a list and making many, many introductory calls. It is a different situation if you are trying to reach one specific prospect or you already have a relationship with that prospect. More on that later in this chapter.

If by chance a prospect does call you back this scenario can put you at a disadvantage. When a prospect returns a phone call, you may not have all the information that you need in front of you; you may be in the middle of other things. And if you are making a lot of introductory calls you may have absolutely no idea of who this person is! That will come though in your voice and put you at great disadvantage. Although it is true that with contact-tracking software you can access your prospect's information fairly quickly you are still at a disadvantage when scrambling for information. You are in a much better position to set the agenda of the telephone call if you make it when you are prepared and ready. While it is also true that if you leave messages you will be able to contact more prospects, your goal should be the quality of your contacts, not merely the quantity. Your call will be far more effective person-to-person. And the more effective you are the higher your "hit" rate will be.

While people with whom you have a relationship should eventually return a telephone call, work on the assumption that no one, on an introductory call, will ever call you back. Even if during the initial contact, a prospect says she will call you back, assume that she will not and always say, "I'll plan on touching base in a couple of weeks *(few days, whatever)* if I haven't heard from you." Few prospects will argue with that. If by chance a prospect does return a call, well, view that as a bonus! Be persistent; call on different days, at different times… You may need to put a lead aside for several weeks or even months and then try again. Never let a lead go… but always put yourself in the position of being able to set the agenda by being the one who initiates the call.

Voice Mail

Voice mail is more and more pervasive and will probably continue to be so. When I started my introductory-calling career, voice mail did not exist. All I had to deal with were the screens. Today many, many calls are answered not by human beings but by machine. This can be frustrating. I do not believe, however, that the overall number of times that one gets through to a prospect has changed significantly. The difference is that those times that you do not reach your prospect, instead of a secretary telling you the prospect is unavailable, you now reach voice mail. Hang up, make another phone call. Remember that it is the quality of the conversation that you have with your prospect, not the number of telephone calls that counts.

The above advice applies when you are working from a list of prospects. It is a different story, however, when there is one specific prospect that you must reach. In that scenario, here are some suggestions for voice mail:

Four Ways To Handle Voice Mail

1. Program your prospect's telephone number into your phone. Call every 10 minutes. Eventually someone will pick up the phone. If they do happen to ask if you have been calling, stay casual and say, "Oh, I've called a few times…" (This hardly ever happens.) Or if you don't feel comfortable calling every 10 minutes, make sure that you call often. Persistence does count. You will eventually get through, long after others have given up.

2. Vary your calling times. If you are only reaching voice mail you have no way of ascertaining when your prospect will be there. Call throughout the day and throughout the week. Try calling early in the morning before the business day begins or after office hours end. Sometimes calling during lunchtime is effective. Often executives who are putting in long hours will answer their telephone during off-hours but not during the day. When you find a time that works for a particular prospect, make a note in your database.

3. Call the extension with one number up or down from your prospect's. Hopefully the person who answers will be someone who is near your prospect and perhaps they can tell your prospect they have a telephone call. Or if

they can't, perhaps they can suggest a good time to call back. If you are calling a smaller company, you can possibly access the information that you need by calling the main company number. Ask whoever answers when is the best time to reach your prospect? Say: "I've been trying to reach Jane Jones—is she in today? When would be the best time to reach her?" You might also give choices of times: "Is late today good or would first thing tomorrow be better?"

4. As a last resort, if you absolutely *must* reach a particular prospect ask if she can be paged.

Make sure that you keep adding leads to the list from which you are working. You do not want to be calling only voice mail numbers over and over again. Rather you want to keep trying those prospects while continuing to add new names to your list.

If You Absolutely, Positively Feel That You Must Leave a Message

Use this as an absolute last resort when you have tried everything and nothing has worked. Do this only if you believe that you must get in touch with *that particular prospect* right away. If you do leave a message, give an abbreviated version of your pitch. When leaving a message, however, do not ask for an appointment in the message. Simply state what you wish to discuss and make sure to say that you will keep trying to reach them.

In your message make sure that you leave your first and last name and your company name. If any of these names are unusual, spell it, s-l-o-w-l-y so that your prospect can write it down. Repeat your telephone number at least twice, once at the beginning of the message and once at the end. And again, say it s-l-o-w-l-y so that your prospect can write it down. Speak clearly and a little slower than normal speech. No one will call you back if they cannot understand your message!

Then do a lot of follow up, possibly send a letter... and keep calling. Persistence counts here.

Other Calls

1. The Confirmation Call.

A confirmation call is an opportunity to "resell" the meeting and to insure that your prospect will be there when you show up. You do not want to waste your time. Assume that your prospect will confirm—they did schedule the meeting in the first place! If for some reason your prospect needs to reschedule, you have them right there on the line, open your calendar and reschedule the meeting. When calling to confirm say: "I'm calling to confirm our meeting at _____." You can also use the guilt technique, adding: "I'm really looking forward to meeting you..." "I've put together the samples we discussed..." "I've thought a lot about your situation..." You get the idea. Once you have confirmed the meeting—get off the telephone! Do not turn this into an extended conversation. Save that for the face-to-face meeting.

I have been to seminars and read books on cold calling where the seminar leaders and/or authors suggest that one not confirm an appointment because you can run the risk of having the prospect cancel. I think this is the wrong way to think about your meeting with your prospect. If you think about your prospect in this manner, the assumption is almost as if you have tricked them and they will be looking for a way to "get out of it." If you are really committed to your integrity and the integrity of your product or service, then this is certainly not a trick.

You should be looking at this process as a benefit to your prospective customer or client. Your prospect may need to reschedule, things do come up, but this is not a cancellation—your prospect is not saying that they do not want to see you, they are merely saying that a particular time is not good. (Remember what they say versus what we hear.) Reschedule the meeting. Sometimes a prospect's situation may change, they are no longer the decision-maker, they are leaving the company... This is also not a cancellation—their situation has changed and they are no longer a viable prospect. (Remember what they say versus what we hear.)

On a confirmation call try to speak directly with your prospect. Use the same persistence here that you used in the initial call. Just keep calling until you reach them. As a last resort leave a message confirming the meeting but ask them to call back to confirm. Usually they do—remember at this point you have established a relationship with this prospect. And again, you do not want to waste your time; you want to make sure they are going to be there. If you do not hear from them, leave another message saying that since you have not heard from them, you are assuming the time is no longer good for them and you will call back to reschedule. Then call back to reschedule. This last scenario actually happens very infrequently. Before leaving a confirmation message ask if a prospect can be paged. Since you have already established a relationship with your prospect you can do this and a confirmation always works better if you are able to speak directly with your prospect.

2. The Rescheduling Call

Always assume that your prospect will reschedule. Remember: they did schedule that initial meeting and unless their situation has changed drastically (they're leaving the job, there's been a reorganization and they are no longer the decision-maker... etc.) most likely the time did not work and you only need to reschedule for a more convenient time. Immediately take the burden off your prospect. Assure her it's okay and right then reschedule for another time. Say: "when would work better for you? One day next week...." Give some options, just as you did when originally scheduling the meeting. Make sure also that you repeat the date and time at least twice s-l-o-w-l-y, directing them with your voice to write it down. Then when the day comes, make sure that you call to confirm. You may have to reschedule a meeting a few times. It happens. Persistence counts here as well.

3. The Follow-Up Call

After you have met with your prospect you want to follow up with them soon. If you have discussed a particular project you will of course talk about that. Even if it was just a general introductory meeting call them anyway. Thank them for the meeting, say " I want to stay in touch, when should I check back with you if I haven't heard from you?" You can also offer suggestions of time "...in a month, in 2 months..." Make reasonable guestimates based on your conversations with the prospect. This way they will tell you how they want you to stay in touch. If your prospect asks you to call back in two weeks, call back in a week and a half. If your prospect asks you to call back in 2 months, call back in six weeks. You always want to be early on a follow-up call. This way you will not miss out on opportunities. Your prospect may ask you to call back yet again, but that's okay. If you feel uncomfortable, that perhaps you are calling too often—ask. Your prospect will tell you. I usually say "I don't want to drive you crazy, when should I call back?" Usually they say "You're not—I appreciate the follow-up!" Then they tell me when to call and of course I call back early.

Two Key Words—Help & Advice

When in doubt, or when having a hard time finding the information that you need use words like "help" and "advice." "Perhaps you can *help* me." "Perhaps you can give me your *advice*." People love to be asked for their help and advice. And they will help! For example, if you have used Example #3 in "Five Ways to Name the Prospect" (Chapter 9) and you have randomly dialed extensions until you reach a human being, say: "Perhaps you can help me. Who is in charge of…"

Four Key Questions

When you need information from your prospect—ask! Here are some samples:

1. "When should I call you back?"
2. "How should I follow up?"
3. "What is the next step?"
4. "Who else is involved in this decision?"

Once you've asked these questions—follow through! Do what you say you are going to do. Persistence counts!

Getting Referrals

Once you have scheduled your meeting, if you think that there may be others in the company who also use your product or service and if you have had a good conversation with your prospect, it is appropriate to ask for a referral. "Who else should I speak with?" Ask if they can join in. Try to arrange things yourself. If there are other prospects within a company, take charge and call those other prospects directly. "Hi, New Prospect! I was just speaking with Jane Jones and we scheduled a brief introductory meeting on (*day*) at (*time*) and she suggested that it would be a good idea for me to introduce myself to you as well." Then go into your pitch. Do not, however, ask for a referral in a situation where you really had to strong-arm yourself in the door. Get off of the telephone after having scheduled the meeting and wait for the face-to-face to ask for that referral. (At the end of a good meeting, if you have not already asked, it is appropriate to ask for a referral: "Who else do you know...")

One opportunity that callers frequently miss is to ask for referrals from those who have turned you down. If you have not been able to schedule a meeting with a particular prospect you can always ask: "Who do you know who may be more in need of our product/service?" It doesn't hurt to ask and you may very well get the referral. The important part is to ask.

The "Drop-By" Appointment

Some prospects have a difficult time scheduling. They seem not to know what they will be doing moment to moment. If this is the case with your prospect, stay very low-key. You don't want them to feel trapped. Make sure that you let them know that you only need 10 minutes of their time. I sometimes say, "I'm not going to camp in your office for the day..." (say this lightly, it's a joke!) Sometimes a prospect will say you can "drop by" and if she is not busy she will see you. In this case, use your prospect's language. Tell her you will "drop by," then ask what time in the near future would work for her, giving her choices of times: "Is this afternoon around 4:00 good or would tomorrow morning around 10:00 work better?" Again stay low-key and casual. Absolutely do not use the word "appointment" or "meeting." If your prospect is a "drop-by" prospect these words will scare her! If the near future is not good for your prospect, tell her you will "be in her neighborhood" at a time in the future that is convenient for you. You can plan to "be in her neighborhood" if the "drop-by" is scheduled. Ask if that is a good time to "drop by." Your prospect will probably tell you it may be okay but you should call to confirm. Do so—and say, "I'm calling to confirm that I'm going to drop by around..." The key here is to speak in your prospect's language.

Summary

☎ It is your job to call your prospect

☎ Handling voice mail:

1. Program your prospect's telephone number into your phone and call every 10 minutes

2. Vary your calling times

3. Call the extension one up or one down from that of your prospect

4. As a last resort: Ask if your prospect can be paged

☎ If you absolutely must leave a message:

1. Leave your first and last name and company name

2. If the names are unusual, spell them s-l-o-w-l-y

3. Repeat your telephone number twice, once at the beginning and once at the end of your message

☎ Confirm every scheduled meeting. It is an opportunity to "resell" the meeting, and also you do not want to waste your time on a cancelled or forgotten meeting

☎ If a meeting needs to be rescheduled, assume that your prospect will reschedule it. Unless their situation has drastically changed there should be no problem

☎ Always follow up your introductory meetings

☎ Key words:

1. Help

2. Advice

☎ Key Questions:

1. "When should I call you back?"

2. "How should I follow up?"

3. "What is the next step?"

4. "Who else is involved in this decision?"

☎ Ask for referrals

☎ If a prospect says that you can "drop by," speak your prospect's language and arrange to "drop by" at a time that is convenient for both of you!

Chapter 14:
The Performance Model

On an introductory call you have about 10 seconds to grab and hold your prospect's attention. After that you probably will not have a second chance. You have a brief amount of time to tap into your prospect's psyche, feelings and desires, and all you really have to do this with is your voice and your words. In a fleeting moment you want to convey an idea, an impression, an emotion. This is a performance. This does not mean that you must be an actor or that this is somehow phony, it simply means that if you think about your introductory call in this manner then the preparatory steps are simple and easy to follow.

If you want your prospect to respond in a certain and favorable way you must be totally focused, at ease, comfortable and one with your message. Part of being comfortable with and increasing your success is a matter of doing it. If you practice before you actually get on the telephone you will be in a much stronger position than if you simply "wing it." You must be prepared, know what you want to accomplish, and know how you plan to present yourself, your product, service and/or company.

The Warm-Up

When you are a ballet dancer, the very first thing that you must do before any class, rehearsal or performance is warm up. You must stretch out and loosen up and get yourself ready and set up so that you can do what you need to do and so that you *do not hurt yourself*. In the same manner, your warm-up for making introductory calls is your preparation—everything that you need to do before you ever get on the telephone—and everything that you need to do so that you *do not hurt yourself*! The warm-up for making introductory calls includes getting set up (Chapter 2) and then developing your strategic marketing plan—the What, Who and Where. What are you selling (Chapter 3)? Who is going to buy it (Chapter 4)? Where will you find them (Chapter 5)? Your preparatory warm-up also includes writing your introductory script along with an answer to every possible objection you may hear (Chapters 6 and 12). You want to be so well prepared that your prospect never asks a question for which you do not have an answer. Then and only then is it time to get on the telephone!

The Rehearsal

Ballet dancers "take class," at least an hour-and-a-half ballet technique class every day, five or six days a week. A ballet class has a set structure with specific steps done in a specific order and with a built-in progression of difficulty of movement. Everyone, whether they are a beginner or a professional dancer, follows the same class structure and does the same type of steps, with the advanced dancer doing variations of the steps that are more complicated than those of the beginner. Every day ballet dancers start *barre* (the warm-up) with *pliés*, followed by *tendus*, followed by *dégagés*. Everyone does this, every day. The teacher is there to watch and explain and give corrections. If a step does not work, if your balance is off or your "line" is wrong, or if you are falling out of a turn the teacher is there to make corrections and help you improve. When you get a correction, however, it is your job to implement it. Sometimes you might also ask a colleague for help and you always, always watch yourself in the big mirror that is at the front of any dance studio. You critique yourself and work until you get it right. Dancing is a process, it does not happen overnight, but instead takes years of work and concentration.

Over the years of taking class every day, day after day, and repeating the same steps in the same order every day, day after day, a ballet dancer builds technique. Technique is habit. You practice the same steps over and over again until you no longer have to think about them. It is just second nature, a part of you. The technique is simply there.

Your rehearsal process for making introductory calls will work in the same manner. When you rehearse your script over and over you are building your technique—your habits that will get you through your introductory calls. If you are prepared, and you work with the material and rehearse it, your telephone pitch and telephone manner will simply become second nature. You will not have to stop and think when a prospect offers an objection. You will know the answer—it will just come out. By the time you start calling you will almost be on auto-pilot. You will know what you want to say and how you are going to say it.

149

Building an introductory calling technique has another great advantage. When you are having a good day, it is very easy to be "on." Technique will give you a way to get yourself "on" when you are having a bad day. Building technique gives you a process to pull yourself together and get to where you need to be to do your work. That "auto-pilot" process will kick in, allowing you to leave your bad day behind.

I think about an introductory call in the same way I think about a dance performance. Any series of steps or sequence of movement has its own phrasing and timing. As a dancer I have to decide which steps are held, which are emphasized, which are moved through quickly, what it is that I want my audience to see and to feel. This discovery is part of the rehearsal process. In your telephone work you need to decide what it is that you want your prospect to hear and also to feel. How will you get them to hear and feel what you want them to hear and feel? Which words will you emphasize? Which words will you move through quickly? This is why working with a tape recorder and also practicing with friends or colleagues is so valuable. Your goal is to draw your listener into your performance, to be so one with the material, focused and committed, that your prospect hears and responds favorably to what you are saying.

The supreme test for a ballerina is 32 *fouettés*. In the last act of the great classical ballets such as *Swan Lake* or *Giselle*, there is always a duet for the two principal dancers. This is called the *Grand Pas de Deux*. This dance is a formula dance, and as part of that formula the ballerina must perform 32 *fouettés*. A *fouetté* is a 360-degree turn on one leg, performed without putting the other leg down, "on your toes," 32 times in a row, without traveling from the spot on the floor where you start out. Your audience also counts, so if you only perform 31 *fouettés* they know!

This is how you learn how to do 32 *fouettés*. It is the common wisdom that in order to "nail" 32 *fouettés* on stage you have to be able to do 64 *fouettés* in class. That is: 64 turns on one leg, in a row, without putting the other leg down, "on your toes" and without traveling from the spot on the floor where you start out. This is how it works: Everyone spreads out in the dance studio and the accompanist starts to play. The music is always a kind of circus-sounding music with a very driving rhythm. You begin to do *fouettés* and you perform one or two and then you fall down. You get up, you perform another one or two *fouettés*, and then you fall down. You get back up, you perform another one or two *fouettés*, and then you fall down. Pretty soon, before you know it, you are performing three *fouettés*—and then you fall down. That is how it works. But what is really marvelous and exciting about this entire process is that if you keep practicing, keep working on your *fouettés* and perfecting your technique—you get better, it gets easier and you can do it! It works exactly the same way with making introductory calls. If you keep working on your introductory calling, you get better, it gets easier and you can do it. Whether it is performing *fouettés* or making introductory calls—no one is simply born knowing how to do it!

Ballet dancers must be tenacious, dedicated, disciplined and hard-working. Training a ballet dancer takes many, many years. Fortunately, learning to make introductory calls is a much shorter process than either learning to perform 32 *fouettés* or becoming a professional ballet dancer! It does, however, require knowledge, patience and persistence. If you are doing something that works for you—keep doing it. If, after you have worked in a certain way for a while, an approach that you are using does not bring the success you want—try something new! Give it some thought, ask a colleague, read books, take seminars…. The point is that you do not quit.

The Performance

When you are dancing your focus must always be "in the moment," you are only thinking about what you are doing right then. You are not looking at the past; you are not looking into the future. You are only in the present. If you are performing and you make a misstep, you deal with it at that moment, and then you go on. This is called focus. Your audience doesn't care that you've made a misstep, they probably don't even notice. Once that step is finished you are on to the next without looking back. The important part is that you stay in the moment, deal with what is happening in the moment and continue to move forward. If you allow yourself to hold onto the mistake, or feelings about the mistake, you will probably just make more mistakes. Sometimes in performance certain steps or certain parts of the choreography can be extremely difficult. If you are anxious about a difficult step that comes later in the choreography, you cannot allow your anxiety about that difficult step to make you lose focus and then misstep on the parts that are not as difficult! This works exactly the same way in sports and in many areas of life, including making introductory calls.

When making introductory calls, you must be there, in that moment with the person to whom you are speaking. If you have had a problem with an earlier call, you must let that problem and the feelings you may have about it go. If you are anxious about being able to schedule a meeting or about the meeting itself, you need to do the work to reduce your anxiety. The best way to do that is to have an awareness of your negative internal dialogue. You do have control of your thoughts and it is your choice to move forward or to hang onto the bad feelings created by your thoughts. Stay in the moment. Don't worry about the future. Don't hold on to the past. Focus on what is happening right now and only on what is happening right now. If you move from moment to moment in this manner, your introductory calling will be much easier and far less stressful.

You may find that you are nervous, afraid or anxious when you first start making introductory calls, and that is perfectly normal—it is called stage fright. In the world of ballet, you take class every day, day after day, week after week, year after year, polishing and perfecting your technique. And it is technique that gets you through stage fright. The more you perform the easier it gets. If you build a solid calling technique it will get you through your calling anxiety. And as you continue to make calls your anxiety and stage fright will diminish—I promise.

Summary

☎ **The Warm-Up**

1. Get set up
2. Develop strategic marketing plan
   ◆ What?
   ◆ Who?
   ◆ Where?
3. Write your script—including answers to objections

☎ **The Rehearsal**

1. Building an introductory calling technique
2. Technique = Habit
3. Making introductory calls is a process
4. Do not quit!

☎ **The Performance**

1. Focus
2. Stay in the moment
3. Technique conquers stage fright

☎ Chapter 15: Tips

Tip #1

The first and most important tip is: **Be yourself.** No one wants to deal with a phony. It is okay to simply be yourself. Be genuine. Now perhaps at this point you will be confused, wanting to know how you can be yourself when you have a prepared script, prepared answers and have been rehearsing. The first part of the answer is that you are selling a product or service in which you believe. That is genuine! The second part of the answer is that the rehearsal process is simply a part of being prepared. In this process you will become comfortable with your presentation and never at a loss for what you are going to say. You will be so well prepared that nothing will phase you. And again, within any good script there needs to be maneuvering room. Just because you have a script does not mean that you stop being a thinking human being. The unexpected can happen. For the most part prospects do respond in a fairly predictable manner—but sometimes they don't. So in addition to knowing your script you must also be ready to respond to the unexpected. This is where active listening comes in. You must focus on the conversation you are having with your prospect and only on that conversation. This, too, is genuine.

Tip #2

Remember to breathe! Sometimes when people get nervous, they forget to breathe. Breathing relaxes and grounds you. Take deep breaths; fill your lungs with air. If you find you have this problem, do some breathing exercises before you pick up the telephone. These exercises can be as simple as closing your eyes and taking deep breaths in and out. Try breathing in for four counts and out for four counts. And focus on your breath. You can also sit in a chair and breathe into each vertebra of your spine. Also try moving around. Move your shoulders, head and arms; shake out your legs. Sometimes you can breathe better if you are standing. Try that. Sometimes pacing while you are talking helps to get energy going and let out the nervous tension—one good reason to have a long cord on your telephone or better yet, a cordless telephone.

While you are calling, try and stay conscious of your breathing. If you find you are feeling stressed and holding your breath, take a moment, do your breathing exercises again and then go on.

Tip #3

Your voice is your instrument on an introductory call. All that you have is your voice, your words and your attitude. To maximize your vocal effect it is often a good idea to *pitch your voice to a lower level than your usual speaking voice*. This is especially important for women. In our society a lower-pitched voice is perceived as more authoritative. It also helps if the inflection at the end of every sentence goes down. When nervous, everyone tends to make even statements into questions with an upward end inflection. This will make you sound nervous and unsure. Be careful as you are doing this, however, not to drop off or throw the last words of your sentence away. This will sound as if you are giving up. If speaking in this manner is difficult, again practice with a tape recorder until the lower pitch of your voice and the downward inflection at ends of sentences is comfortable. (There are occasional exceptions to this rule of the downward inflection, for example when a prospect makes a "never" statement as in "I never make appointments." Your response "Never?" should have an upward inflection. But these cases really are the exceptions.)

Tip #4

The emphasis on a particular word can totally change the meaning of a sentence. For example, let's take the phrase "She is not a thief." If you emphasize the "She"—"*She* is not a thief"—the sentence means that she is not a thief, but someone else is. If you emphasize "not"—"She is *not* a thief"—the sentence is a defense. If you emphasize "thief"— "She is not a *thief*"—the sentence implies that she is something else that you have just not named. Think about the emphasis that you wish to make.

Tip #5

As a dancer, I believe strongly in the power of rhythm. Everyone has his or her own personal rhythm, the tempo at which he or she thinks and functions and is most comfortable. People generally have a difficult time with people whose rhythms are different from their own. Think

157

about it—if you speak quickly—do you find yourself getting impatient with someone who speaks at a much slower pace? Do you perceive them as dull, perhaps not too bright? On the other hand, if you have a more laid-back rhythm to your speech, do you find people who speak quickly annoying and difficult to deal with? This is very common. People can grasp your message much more effectively if it is delivered in a rhythm that matches their own. Remember, your goal is communication. Therefore try to *follow your prospect's rhythm*. Match your timing and tempo to theirs. You can even try and match their volume. This will aid in their ability to hear and understand you. If you find this to be difficult, again try practicing with a colleague or friend.

Tip #6

If you are having difficulty getting into a "conversational rhythm" with your script try *deliberately speeding up at the beginning and end of sentences and slowing down in the middle*. This will give your delivery a more conversational feel along with the added benefit of making it more difficult for your prospect to interrupt you. People will generally interrupt at the end of a sentence. By speeding up at that time your prospect will not hear a place to jump in.

Tip #7

When you get to the really important part of your script try whispering. This focuses your prospect's attention because they will be concentrating on listening and this also helps to draw them into your performance. It's enticing. Make sure, however, that you do not whisper so much that they cannot hear you but just enough to draw your prospect in. Repetition of words can have the same effect. Example: "This is a very,

very exciting new product." The word "very" repeated twice, spoken slowly and with emphasis can have an almost hypnotic effect.

Tip #8

When a prospect puts you on a speakerphone, again try whispering. They'll more than likely pick up the receiver so that they can hear you.

Tip #9

People buy from people they like and people with whom they are comfortable. In the same way, your prospects schedule meetings with people with whom they like and are comfortable. So be courteous, be genuine, and listen! *Give your prospect your complete attention.* When your prospect tells you of her concerns try to repeat them back to her. This does two things, it shows your prospect that you are listening and it makes sure that you get it right! If you do not, your prospect can correct you and then you will get it right!

Tip #10

Think of your prospect as someone you know, someone who is open and interested.

Tip #11

Use directed words. For example when you ask to speak with your prospect say: "Jane Jones, please." and not "May I speak with Jane Jones?" The first sentence conveys authority, the second asks permission. Another example: ask "Whom should I speak with?" and not "Do you know whom I should speak with?" Again, the first conveys authority and whomever you are questioning, if they know, must answer with a name.

In the second sentence the response could simply be "yes" or "no."

Tip #12

Whether trying to ascertain a good time to call your prospect back or trying to schedule a meeting, it is a good idea to *give alternate choices.* "Is this afternoon good or would tomorrow morning be better?" It is much easier for your prospect to decide when rather than whether.

Tip #13

Call when the prospect is in. Call when you know you can reach the prospect. Early, late, lunchtime…. Your industry may have times that are specific to that industry. Call when the secretary said to call back.

Tip #14

Keep adding new telephone numbers to your list. You do not want to keep calling the same numbers over and over. You want to keep adding telephone numbers so that you are calling a mix of new leads and older leads.

Tip #15

If you keep reaching a secretary or assistant, do not call that lead more than 3 times in one day. This is one reason to keep adding new names to your list. If you keep reaching voice mail, however, you can call as often as you wish.

Tip #16

Write everything down—or enter the information in your database! The better your records the easier your calls will be.

Tip #17

If you are put on hold at the switchboard, go on to another call. If you are actually holding for your prospect and you've been on hold for a while, you can hang up then call back. Say "I was holding for (*prospect's name*) and I was disconnected—Is she available?" This way you'll either get through to your prospect or find out when to call back.

Tip #18

If you are setting up meetings for someone else, you can say things about that individual that they themselves cannot. Don't be afraid to gush. Point out all relevant personality traits; "She is so talented," "She is so down-to-earth," "She really understands this business." You get the idea. Coming from a second party these types of statements are very powerful. If you say them about yourself, however, you simply sound like a braggart.

Tip #19

If you are trying to name the prospect and you reach an automated telephone answering system, the type that is sometimes used to replace the receptionists (dial 1 for this, 2 for that...), *try to find a way to reach a human being.* Dial 0 for Operator and try, "Before you connect me..." or randomly dial numbers until you reach a person. Identify yourself and say, "I'm hoping you can help me... I need to reach... Who would that be?"

Tip #20

After a success, keep calling!

Tip #21

Take breaks when you need them. There is no sense in blowing leads simply because you are tired. You must, of course, distinguish between a legitimate need for a break and just trying to put off making calls.

Tip #22

Be Persistent!—Keep making telephone calls.

Chapter 16:
Don't Do This!
Common Mistakes

1. Do not tell all to the receptionist or secretary

Remember, your best bet to name the decision-maker and/or get through to that decision-maker is to remain undercover. Your business is with the decision-maker, and only the decision-maker.

Do use screening techniques to stay undercover until you get your prospect on the telephone

2. Do not ask your prospect "How are you today?"

Generally they will answer "I am fine, what do you want?" This immediately starts your conversation off on the wrong foot.

Do identify yourself and your company and start your pitch. If this is not a good time, your prospect will let you know

3. Do not ask, "May I have a moment of your time?"

Generally your prospect will answer "What do you want?" again starting your conversation off on the wrong foot.

Do assume the time is ok. If it is not, your prospect will let you know

4. Do not ask, "Are you the person who purchases...?"

Again your answer will probably be "What do you want?"

Do allow your prospect to self-qualify. Give the prospect your pitch and let her tell you that she is the decision-maker. If you are still not sure ask, "Who else is involved in this decision?"

5. Do not argue with your prospect or tell her that she is wrong

If your prospect is uninterested or will not schedule a meeting at this time, do not tell her she is stupid, misguided or just plain wrong.

Do remember your prospect's priorities and your priorities are bound to be different. If you leave your conversation on a good note you can continue to stay in touch and perhaps the situation will change. If you have an argument with your prospect, chances are you will never get in to see her

6. Do not leave messages

Do not expect that anyone will ever call you back. It is your job to get in touch with your prospect. If someone does return a phone call—consider that to be a bonus!

Do be persistent in pursuing your prospect

7. Do not stay undercover with your prospect

Stay undercover with the receptionist and/or secretary. Once you have your prospect on the telephone:

Do clearly identify yourself and your company

8. Do not read your script word for word like a canned presentation

No one wants to speak with someone who is reading a script. This is why the rehearsal process is so important.

Do be prepared and talk like a person!

9. Never put your prospect on hold

Do you like being put on hold? You'll lose your prospect this way.

Do give your prospect your complete attention

10. Don't have call waiting

Do you like call waiting? Do you like being put on hold? You'll lose your prospect this way.

Do focus on your prospect

11. Don't be stumped by prospect objections

You've done your homework, you're reading this book, don't be caught unprepared. If there are prospect objections that are unique to your industry or if a prospect voices an objection that you have not heard before, take the time to work out the answers. Then try those answers out until you find an answer that works. Be creative.

Do be ready with your responses to a prospect's objections

12. Do not project your own fears and insecurities onto your prospect

Do listen actively to your prospect and respond to what she is actually saying

13. Do not pitch only what interests you

This process is about your prospect, not about you. Remember that people buy for their reasons, not yours.

Do pitch to your prospect's concerns

14. Do not get defensive with your prospect or take things personally

This is not personal, this is sales. A "no" is not a personal rejection. You have no way of knowing exactly what is going on with your prospect. She may just be having a bad day. You could call her again in a couple of months and her situation and attitude may have completely changed.

Do move on

15. Do not stop making telephone calls

The biggest mistake that you can make when prospecting for new business is to stop. There is no new business without prospecting! You have done your homework, you are reading this book, and your "hit" rate is going to improve! I promise. Now is the time to make even more phone calls and garner even more success. The more calls you make, the more success you will have. The more doors you open, the more sales you will close.

Do keep calling!

Chapter 17:
Abducted by Aliens?

There are situations where it is imperative to reach a particular prospect at a particular time. This could happen on an introductory call where you believe the timing is crucial. Maybe there is a narrow window of opportunity because of a recent development in business or technology and you want to exploit it. If you do not reach your prospect within a certain amount of time, you believe the opportunity will be lost. Or maybe instead, this is a follow-up call. You are trying to reach a prospect to continue a conversation, timing is all, and you are having no success reaching her. In either of these scenarios, you have tried everything. You have called repeatedly at different times throughout the day; you have even left messages. All with no response.

I offer here a last-resort letter. I am indebted to Mitch Turner for this idea. He has been using this for years. I have also started using a version of this letter—only as a last resort—when I have been unable to reach a prospect and the response rate has been high. When all else fails, try this letter:

April 1, 2001

Ms. Jane Jones
ABC Company
123 Main Street
Anywhere, USA

Dear Ms. Jones:

You may not know this, but I have been attempting to reach you, almost on a daily basis, for some time now, with no success. You are never available when I call, and clearly, you have been unable to return my phone calls. I am worried about you.

Have you been abducted by aliens?

If you have, and can somehow use the enclosed, pre-addressed, stamped envelope to notify me, I will notify the Coast Guard and alert the media and do everything in my power to obtain your release.

If, however, the problem is limited to a demanding schedule, I am writing to encourage you to call me when you have a free moment. Hopefully, the information I am enclosing will justify that call.

> *(Information about your company,*
> *product or service goes here.)*

Don't you agree that if we can show you (*Customer Benefit goes here*), your time will have been well spent?

It would be nice to hear from you.

Sincerely,

Wendy Weiss

With your letter, enclose a response card, something like this:

Ms. Wendy Weiss
D.F.D. Publications, Inc.
P.O. Box 20664
London Terrace Station
New York, NY 10011

Dear Wendy:

You are right!

PLEASE CHECK APROPRIATE BOX

❑ Help! I have been abducted by aliens! Please do whatever you can to rescue me!

❑ I have not been abducted by aliens. The next time you call, I will be available. I am looking forward to speaking with you!

❑ The best time to reach me is _____ at _____.
                                      (day)   (time)

Please call me then. I am looking forward to speaking with you!

Sincerely,

Jane Jones

Make sure you include a stamped, self-addressed envelope with your reply card.

I have found that upon receipt of this letter, prospects frequently call me. If however, you do not hear from your prospect within 8 to 10 business days, call to follow up.

Use this letter as a last resort—you can, after all, use this only once with any given prospect. If you can simply reach your prospect by telephone, it is a one-step process and much more effective. You can say what you need to say, get an answer and then move on.

Chapter 18:
How Many Calls Will I Have to Make?

The answer to this starts with the question—How much money do you want to make? First you must determine your income objective. Let's say that you want to make $100,000 this year. (For these calculations I am assuming *no* past customers and *no* repeat business. Introductory calling will generate every dollar—the reality will be easier!) Next you must look at the average cost per unit of sale. In other words, what is the average cost of your product or service, or if you are working on commission what is your average commission? Divide your income objective by that average cost or commission to come up with the number of sales you will need.

Income objective ÷ average cost or commission = number of sales

Let's say that your average cost per unit of sale is $1,000. $100,000 divided by $1,000 equals 100. You now know that you will need to close 100 sales to make $100,000.

$100,000 ÷ $1,000 = 100 sales

Next, determine your average sale rate per lead. How many viable, qualified leads or prospects must you contact before you close one sale? This number, like average cost, will vary from person to person, product to product.

Qualified lead-to-sale ratio

If you generally turn 1 out of 5 new qualified prospects into a new customer, then you know that you will need 5 qualified prospects to make one sale.

5 qualified leads to make 1 sale

Multiply your number of qualified leads—5—by the number of sales that you need—100.

Qualified leads x number of sales

Now you know that you will need 500 qualified leads in one year to make 100 sales to then make $100,000.

5 qualified leads x 100 sales = 500 qualified leads needed

Next, determine the average number of calls (that is how many times you dial the phone) it will take you to get those leads.

 # dials-to-one genuine lead ratio

Let's say that you need to make 10 calls to find one genuine lead.

10 dials to one genuine lead

Multiply those 10 calls by your number of leads—500— to get the total number of calls you will need to make—5,000 calls in a year to generate 500 qualified leads to close 100 sales to make $100,000.

10 calls x 500 leads = 5,000 calls

If you want to know how many calls that is per week, take the 5,000 calls and divide them by the number of weeks you work, lets say 50 (I'm giving you two weeks for vacation). That comes to 100 calls per week.

 # calls ÷ weeks in year = # calls per week

5000 calls ÷ 50 weeks = 100 calls per week

Divide that number by the 5 days in the work week and you will find that you only need to dial the telephone a mere 20 calls a day to generate enough new business to earn $100,000.

100 calls ÷ 5 days = 20 calls per day

The biggest obstacles here are keeping the records, which a lot of people (myself included) dislike doing, and then following through on the plan and making those 20 calls per day. Without accurate records you cannot devise your plan and without follow-through, your plan is worthless. Remember that these numbers are averages, so you need to stick to the plan for the plan to work. Set a time every day to make calls, and then do it! Also, as you continue calling, your skills will improve. Your "hit" rate for new leads and closing sales will go up. You might have to make fewer calls to get the qualified leads that you need. In addition, if you increase the number of calls in your plan, your sales and earnings will increase in direct proportion to the amount that you increase your introductory calls.

Think about these numbers. If you are making 5,000 calls a year, how important is any one phone call or any one lead? If you get a voice mail instead of a person, you have 4,999 more chances! If someone says "no" to you, you have 4,998 more chances! This is a great way of keeping it all in perspective.

Another way to think about these numbers: If someone were to fill your bathtub with 1,000 marbles, and if on only one marble there was a black dot that made the marble worth $10,000, would you go through all of those marbles to find the one worth $10,000? Of course you would! Each of those 1,000 marbles is worth $10 to you if you go through all of the marbles and find the one with the black dot. If you stop before you have found that marble with the dot, then all of the marbles are worthless.

Below is a chart to help you track your calls. You need to track your "dials completed," that is, the number of times that you dial the telephone. You want to track both introductory calls and follow-up calls. You must also track your "completed calls," calls when you actually speak with the decision-maker. Again, track introductory calls and follow-up calls. Track your number of sales, the number of prospects you must call back and the number of prospects that turned out to not be viable.

Tracking Your Calls

Dials Completed:

  Number of Introductory Calls

  Number of Follow-Up Calls

Completed Calls:

  Number of Introductory Calls

  Number of Follow-Up Calls

Results:

  Number of Sales

  Needs Information/Call-Back/Pending

  Not Viable

Tracking the Averages

Your Average Commission:

Your Average Ratio: dials to leads

Your Average Ratio: leads to sales

Example:

Income objective:	$100,000/year
Average cost per unit of sale:	$1,000
Income objective ÷ cost per unit:	100 sales needed
Qualified lead-to-sale ratio:	5 to 1
Qualified leads x sales:	500 qualified leads
Ratio of dials to qualified lead:	10 to 1
Dials x leads:	5,000 dials/year
Dials ÷ weeks:	100 dials/week
Dials ÷ day:	20 dials/day

Your Numbers:

Income objective:

Average cost per unit of sale:

Income objective ÷ cost per unit:

Qualified lead-to-sale ratio:

Qualified leads x sales:

Ratio of dials to qualified leads:

Dials x leads:

Dials ÷ weeks:

Dials ÷ day:

Chapter 19:
Let's Make an Appointment!

The Game

I like to think of introductory calling as a game—it's called *"Let's Make an Appointment!"* It's a game of skill, daring and numbers with a lot of room for creativity and self-expression. And it can be fun. It is affirming to hear people say "yes." Like any game, however, there are rules, and you need to know them and follow them. The rules are listed below. They are simple and easy to follow. The rules cover most situations— but occasionally they don't. That's why you need to know when to play a hunch and/or follow your intuition. Like a sport, the more you practice the better you get. And persistence does count! Simply put, the more calls you make, the more success you will have.

If introductory calling does not come easily, take a course, talk to others who do a lot of introductory calling, talk to colleagues and other salespeople, ask for their help and advice. And make telephone calls.

Ultimately, however, introductory calling is a game. It is not life or death; the fate of the world does not rest on you and your telephone. You will not destroy your company or ruin your life if a prospect says "no." It's only a call. Loosen up, play the game, have some fun.

The Rules

1. *Prepare*

   Do your homework. Set up your strategic marketing plan. Know your selling points and customer benefits. Set up your system. Write your script. Practice, practice, practice!

2. *Work from the top down*

   Call the highest-level person who you think is the decision-maker.

3. *Ask for what you want*

4. *Be persistent*

5. *Don't leave messages*

   No one will ever call you back. Getting hold of the prospect is your job.

6. *Every prospect pretty much says the same thing—sometimes they don't*

7. *After a success keep calling*

8. *Stay calm*

   You will for the most part be talking to people who will appreciate your call. If a prospect is rude, remember: This is not personal. Move on.

9. *Listen to your prospect*

10. *Be yourself*

11. *Have fun*

12. *Keep calling*

Glossary of Terms

Benefit	The reason your customer or client purchases your product or service.
Big Benefit	What your prospect is *really* purchasing. Things like financial stability, love, recognition, independence.... These are basic human desires.
Buy Into	Believing in and being 100% committed to the value of your product or service.
Closing	Asking for what you want and/or getting what you want.

Cold Call	*(noun) (The American Heritage® Dictionary of the English Language, Third Edition* ©1996) A telephone call or visit made to someone who is not known or not expecting contact, often in order to sell something.
Completed Calls	The number of calls when you speak directly with the prospect (not the secretary, assistant or voice mail).
Completed Dials	The number of times you dial the telephone.
Customer/Client Benefits	How your customer or client will be better off after purchasing your product or service.
Decision-Maker	The person who can actually make the decision to purchase your product or service. Not a secretary, not someone who says they need to speak with their boss. Someone who does not need any other authorization.
Features	Characteristics, facts or specifications that are innate to your product or service. They are just "there."

Hit	Making an appointment. Closing.
Hook	Whatever grabs your prospect's attention and interest.
Introductory Call	I prefer this to the term "cold call." You are calling to introduce yourself, your product or service, your company.
Lead	*(noun)* Prospect. The person you are calling, the person you want to reach.
List Broker	Intermediary who works as a liaison between the list owner or manager and the list renter. The list broker works primarily for the list renter.
List Owner	Private company, organization or marketer that has its own in-house lists which are made available for rental.
List Manager	Administers, manages and markets lists for many different list owners. List managers work primarily for the list owner.
Performance	The actual introductory call.

Pitch	*(noun)* Your script, what you say. *(verb)* To deliver your script to a prospect, to 'pitch' a prospect.
Product	Generally, what you are selling.
Projection	Your own insecurities and fears which you assume that your prospect shares and which you see reflected back to you.
Prospect	The person to whom you are selling.
Qualified Lead	A lead that meets your pre-selected criteria.
Qualify	Making sure that the prospect to whom you are speaking really is in a position to make the decision to purchase your product or service. Making sure that your prospect meets your pre-selected criteria.
Qualifying Parameters	Your pre-selected criteria. The conditions that are necessary for you to consider doing business with a prospect.
Qualifying Questions	Predetermined questions which, when asked of your prospect, help to determine whether or not that prospect really is a viable prospect.

Screen

Secretary, receptionist, assistant... anyone who stands between you and your prospect (also sometimes referred to as a "gatekeeper").

Script

An outline of what you plan to say which includes answers to objections.

Self-qualify

Allowing the decision-maker to identify themselves.

Sell

(verb) (The American Heritage® Dictionary of the English Language, Third Edition ©1996) To persuade (another) to recognize the worth or desirability of....

Selling Points

Information about your product that is of interest to and will help to "sell" your prospect.

Sound Bite

One sentence, which expresses clearly and succinctly what you do.

 **Resources**

Berkley, Susan, *Speak to Influence, How to Unlock the Hidden Power of Your Voice*. New Jersey: Campbell Hall Press, 1999.

Bly, Robert W., *Secrets of Successful Telephone Selling*. New York: Henry Holt and Company, 1997.

Burns, David D., M.D., *Feeling Good, The New Mood Therapy*. New York: William Morrow and Company, 1980.

Cialdini, Robert B., *Influence: The Psychology of Persuasion*. New York: Quill William Morrow, 1993.

Dimitrius, Jo-Ellan, Ph.D., and Mazarella, Mark, *Reading People*. New York: Ballantine Books, 1998, 1999.

Elgin, Suzette Haden, *Success with the Gentle Art of Verbal Self Defense*. New Jersey: Prentice Hall, 1989.

Girard, Joe, *How to Close Every Sale*. New York: Warner Books, 1989.

Gitomer, Jeffrey H., *The Sales Bible*. New York: William Morrow and Company, Inc., 1994.

Gleeck, Fred, *30 Days to Better Telephone Technique*, Video.

Gleeck, Fred, *24 Quick and Easy Ways to Radically Improve Customer Service*, Video.

Kennedy, Danielle, *Balancing Acts: An Inspirational Guide for Working Mothers*. New York: Penguin Putnam, 1998.

Kennedy, Danielle, *Seven-Figure Selling*. New York: Penguin Putnam, 1996.

Ringer, Robert J., *Winning Through Intimidation*. New York: Fawcett Crest Books, 1974.

Sun Tzu, *The Art of War*. New York: Oxford University Press, 1963.

Walters, Dottie, *Never Underestimate the Selling Power of a Woman*. North Hollywood, CA: Wilshire Book Company, 1983.

Walters, Dottie, and Laaman, Laura, *Selling Women*, Audio Album.

Walters, Dottie, and Walters, Lilly, *Speak & Grow Rich*. New Jersey: Prentice Hall, Inc., 1997.

About the Author

Wendy Weiss is a consultant, speaker and author specializing in new-business development and cold calling. Since 1988 she has worked with a wide range of businesses in New York City in fields as diverse as the graphic arts and financial services, cold calling and setting appointments for her clients to expand their customer base. In addition to creating Weiss Communications, Wendy is the founding director of Illusion Productions, a not-for-profit dance company providing AIDS education to youth in New York City.

Wendy wrote *Cold Calling for Women: Opening Doors & Closing Sales* to help women overcome their fear of cold calling and to give specific, practical how-to information. Wendy teaches at the Seminar Center in New York City and has trained many sales people and entrepreneurs in the techniques that she has developed.

Wendy is also a former ballet dancer who performed with Pittsburgh Ballet Theater. She got into her current field, sales training, by accident—she needed a "day job." But the results have been happy, and she has no regrets!

Wanted: Practical Sales Training

Wendy Weiss is available for consulting and personal coaching on a one-to-one basis both in New York City and nationwide.

Wendy also offers cold-calling workshops and seminars. Because every industry has its own unique and specific issues, we are happy to adjust our workshops and seminars to your needs and time constraints.

For information about personal coaching, consulting or booking a workshop or seminar, contact Wendy through:

D.F.D. Publications, Inc.
P.O. Box 20664
London Terrace Station
New York, NY 10011
(212) 463-8212
email: wendy@wendyweiss.com
www.wendyweiss.com

Free Offer!

Subscribe to *Opening Doors & Closing Sales,* the free, monthly e-mail newsletter that is packed with tips to develop new business. Visit http://www.wendyweiss.com.

Cold Calling College

Once you have read *Cold Calling for Women* and put the *Performance Model* into action, you may still find that you need additional help. That's not unusual. Few people are naturally gifted at cold calling. Most will never be good without a little help.

I am sure that once you get in to see your prospect, you do a fairly good job of closing them. Wouldn't it be great if you could <u>double</u> or even <u>triple</u> the number of new business appointments you set?

You've taken the first; you've read *Cold Calling for Women*. Step two: ***Cold Calling College***, a proven business-building tool, is available for you today.

Hone your skills with this easy-to-use self-study product. ***Cold Calling College*** begins where *Cold Calling for Women* leaves off. The comprehensive workbook walks you though the process and audio CD's help you polish your delivery. And the best part: ***Cold Calling College*** is available to you whenever you want to use it, late at night, early in the morning, or anytime at all. No clearing your schedule to attend a teleseminar or traveling long distances to participate in a seminar. Simply hit "play" for the CD's and open the workbook, any time and any place of your choice.

To order this sales-enhancing product visit: http://www.wendyweiss.com or call our toll-free number, 866-405-8212 or use the order form on the next page.

Order Form

# copies		Total
_____ *Cold Calling for Women* (book) @ $15.95		$_____
_____ *Cold Calling College,* (audio CD's and workbook) @ $250.00		$_____
Shipping & Handling ($5 first book, $1 each additional, *Cold Calling College*, $10) (Overseas & Canada, call for rates)		$_____
Subtotal		$_____
NYS residents, please add sales tax		$_____
Total Order		$_____

Name _____

Address _____

City _____ State _____ Zip _____

Phone _____

E-mail _____

❑ Check enclosed (check # _____)

❑ Visa ❑ MasterCard ❑ American Express ❑ Discover

Card # _____

Expiration Date _____

Name on Card _____

Signature _____